Circles In The Sand

Circles In The Sand

Living And Working With Wild Animals

Terry Lee Moore

To order additional copies of this book, contact:
Xlibris Corporation
1-888-795-4274
www.Xlibris.com
Orders@Xlibris.com
65739

Contents

I DIDN'T BELIEVE that the sleek 250-pound black jaguar was a man-eater. This was his fourth film, and thus far, Bear had behaved quite well. But after plunging his three-inch-long canines into my leg, I began to reconsider. As an exotic-animal trainer, I knew there were inherent risks in working with wild animals; this time I wasn't lucky.

Circles in the Sand is a book of episodic tales set in various recesses of the dusty desert arroyo, the mountain meadow, the plains and savannas of East Africa. Each tale focuses on a different kind of animal – serpent, tiger, wolf, bear, puma, camel. These tales describe the inevitable risk and sometimes tragic loss that inevitably accompanies the sort of path I have chosen. It is also about overcoming seemingly insurmountable obstacles while following a dream even when it took me to the ends of the earth and occasionally nearly cost my life.

Through all these adventures, I maintained the belief that civilization was ready once more to embrace our environment and the animals that live there. With the rise of industrialization and technology, some of the interest was lost, but I believe a return to the earth and all it has to offer is occurring. This return completes the circle.

The interest to the reader is in my unique journey in relation to ecosystems and the wildlife within them. My purpose is to inspire readers to slow their hurried pace and to walk quietly with me in order to reconnect to the natural world, our original home. It is also to awaken a passion to seek a new path that ensures the survival of the fascinating creatures living in the wild places, including humans.

I attended Gentle Jungle exotic animal training school in 1977 and pursued a twenty-five-year career not only as a trainer but also as a stunt double in movies. I was a stand-in for actors like Michael J. Fox in *Back to the Future III*, James Keach in *The New Swiss Family Robinson*, Jared Rushton in *A Cry in the Wild*, and others.

I have worked as an animal handler for television programs and movies like *The Johnny Carson Show*, *The Jungle Book: Mowgli's Story*, *Anaconda*, and *Deep Impact*. I also owned and operated the only camel trekking business in the United States, which offered camel rides to visitors who came from as far as Mongolia. All along the way, I was involved in wildlife education and rehabilitation.

I am currently working in the education department at Out of Africa Wildlife Park in Sedona Arizona.

Foreword

BY DESIGN, ALL things in the natural world return to where they once began; and in nature, this continuation perpetuates life. From the cylindrical womb comes new life; and with death, one circle ends, granting space for new life to begin. In the dusty desert arroyo or the mountain meadow to the savannas of East Africa, a story unfolds. This story is about life's journeys.

Creatures both great and small, each fulfill their purpose in making the circle whole. Their tracks or circles in the sand have remained virtually unchanged for thousands of years, and a fascinating story lies within. Humankind was once an intricate part of nature's master plan, and we lived within its boundaries. We were both predator and prey, and the world that sustained us took nourishment from us as well when our own cycle ended. With the advent of technology, changes occurred that changed our role with nature and all living things. But an interesting paradigm is now unfolding. Humans are now embracing the earth and returning in record numbers to reconnect with the natural world.

This is the story of one blessed individual that has spent a lifetime surrounded by the creatures that share this sphere of life that we call Earth. It is my dream that the short stories contained within will inspire some to slow their hurried pace and to walk quietly to discover the natural world while basking in the sights and sounds that were once our very beginning. The joys and sorrows of my own life's journey and the four-legged, furry, feathered, and scaly creatures that allowed me to share their space have and will continue to return me to the wild places and seek out the next chapter. I hope you will enjoy this story, and in some way, it touches the wild spirit that dwells within us all.

For although I have yet to be granted an audience with "God"
I feel certain that he still must exist.
For on countless sunlit summer mornings,
I have been privelaged to caress his savage miracles.
With trembling, sweat soaked palms pausing briefly on a glistening, silky coat.
I felt their beating hearts.

The Lessons of Julius Crush

WHEN I WAS only seven years old, I discovered my true passion in life and pursued it in earnest. The year was 1960, which sounds like a lifetime ago, which indeed it was. Although on rare occasions I have trouble remembering my own phone number, there is one treasured memory that I shall never forget. The adventures began on a well-worn trail in a small canyon behind our state capitol building in Salt Lake City, Utah.

I entered the small sunlit clearing that seemed unusually quiet that morning. Even the songbirds had ceased their endless chattering. There in the dappled shadows of the towering aspens and cottonwoods, a faint movement caught my eye. It was a snake. Its glistening yellow-and-black coils firmly held a struggling ground squirrel. While I stood there transfixed, the hapless rodent took its final breath. Caught up in the life-and-death struggle before me, I remained motionless, but the snake was well aware of my presence.

Momentarily, it released its now-lifeless victim. The serpent swiveled its head in my direction all the while flickering its tongue in and out, trying to identify the intruder interrupting its meal. Somehow sensing I was in no way a threat, the powerful constrictor soon located the head of the squirrel and began the long, slow process of swallowing its meal whole. Although the rodent was almost twice the girth of the snake, the unique ability of the snakes to open their jaws a full 180 degrees allows them to consume a large meal. Inch by inch, one giant mouthful at a time, the hefty rodent was eventually devoured. The snake's skin appeared almost paper-thin when its meal was at last consumed. With the task complete, there was one final, exaggerated yawn. The satiated serpent now stretched to its full seven-foot length in order to begin the three-week ordeal of digesting such a large meal.

It was at that point I became aware of another watcher perched in a nearby tree. A large red-tailed hawk was partially concealed in the foliage and was preparing for an aerial assault. The bird ruffled its feathers and glared down at its target below. The focus of her intense stare made her intentions quite obvious. One appetizer and one entrée were now neatly wrapped. What was once the hunter would soon become the victim. The snake was unaware of the predatory bird watching its every movement. With her razor-sharp beak and powerful talons, the hawk would have little difficulty dispatching the now-sluggish snake. But there was one small but influential obstacle standing in her way.

The hungry red-tail had not anticipated a meddlesome seven-year-old running interference on her intended target, though her decision had already been made. Without considering the consequences of my foolish actions, I dashed forward, scooping the startled snake into my arms and ran for the shelter of the nearby forest. The startled serpent wrapped its tail firmly around my arm and exhaled a long and threatening hiss. But to my surprise and great relief, it made no attempt to bite.

That capture would be the first of many. But as I grew older, I would perfect my techniques of serpent wrangling. Today I have successfully captured hundreds of snakes from all around the world. It never ceases to amaze me that one of mankind's most hated and feared adversaries is also a species that, if left alone, poses little or no threat to us whatsoever.

*   *   *

I returned home with my prize. In spite of strenuous objections from my two unreasonable sisters, I was permitted to keep the snake for the remainder of the summer. In time, they grew fond of the gentle, but somewhat unusual, family pet. It was the creepy-crawlies that followed in the years to come that would be far less welcome. Sadly, life as we knew it was about to take a radical change – a change that would forever disrupt our once-peaceful and harmonious existence.

*   *   *

Julius Crush, as he came to be known, was returned in late fall to the canyon where he was captured. His home was changing however as the small once-secluded canyon became a favorite destination for a growing human population of hikers, bikers, joggers, and dog walkers. The docile and trusting snake would forever leave a lasting impression on my very soul that would affect my life from that day forward. But in my child's mind, the canyon called Memory Grove would remain a safe and bountiful haven for Julius. A sacred place protected by dragons and wizards and mythological creatures that can only exist in a world of make-believe: a quiet, sacred place where innocence is bliss and serpents are neither good nor evil. Like a young man's first true love, Julius will never be forgotten.

*   *   *

Since then, I have had countless encounters with a variety of different reptiles from the deserts in the southwest United States to the steamy, impenetrable jungles of Central and South America. From a cobra in Karachi, Pakistan, to a Western diamondback rattlesnakes in Tombstone, Arizona, every encounter has been an exciting and memorable adventure. Snakes, for whatever reason, have always left me with a sense of awe. They have both inspired me and lured me to distant lands. It was the circle of the serpent that slowed my hurried pace and awakened my senses to the possibility of yet another chance encounter with a golden snake that would grace me with its humble presence.

*   *   *

I have never fully understood why humans refer to one well-known phobia as "a natural fear of snakes." Even as an infant, I would have eagerly crawled through an entire room full of snakes without so much as a whimper. I would, however, cry a river of tears at the sound of a blaring car horn or loud voices raised in anger.

At many of the wildlife education programs I conducted at school programs around the West, only children that were taught to fear snakes ran from the room or trembled in fear. Those same adults who teach their offspring to fear snakes will often defy real danger at the drop of a hat. While river rafting on the Colorado River in the summer of 1992, a man and his wife, accompanied by their three small children, refused to exit the raft for fear of seeing a snake. They even slept on board rather than face the possibility of encountering a harmless garter snake on the sandy beach. Many of those adventurous souls enjoyed the insanely dangerous sport of base jumping (jumping from a two-thousand-foot cliff with a parachute) but are far more concerned about being bit by a rattlesnake than splattering on the rocks below them if their parachute fails to open.

I vividly remember one such individual and his totally unnatural fear of snakes. This is his story.

*   *   *

Cobalt Blue

CHARLIE CLARK WAS a "real man" in every sense of the word. Raised on a cattle ranch in Montana, Charlie was a dyed-in-the-wool cowboy. He rode, he roped, and he feared neither man nor beast. By eighteen years of age, Charlie was an accomplished bull rider that had been bucked off, run down, kicked, stomped, gored, and trampled by more hoof stock than most men dreamed of. His remarkable abilities with animals eventually led him to pursue a career as a Hollywood stuntman. It was there I would get to know Charlie and witness firsthand the Achilles' heel of this legendary man.

I was working on a movie set in northern Colorado. The working name of the film was *Desperado*. I was hired as a stand-in for Mr. Clark due to his horrible aversion to snakes . . . especially rattlesnakes. Even the word *snake* sent shivers down this normally fearless man's spine.

The film had a typical Western theme for that era. Cowboy rides horse. Cowboy sees rattlesnake. Cowboy catches, kills, and eats rattlesnake. But this cowboy wasn't getting anywhere near a snake, so I was hired as Charlie's stunt double. I dressed up in my Hollywood cowboy attire complete with boots, hat, spurs, and chaps. The snake was a five-foot-long heavy-bodied southern Pacific rattlesnake named Cobalt. I found Cobalt two years previously in the San Bernardino Mountains near the small town of Wrightwood, California. Cobalt needed to be relocated before he became a hatband, and it was my great pleasure to be his acquaintance.

A young couple from Los Angeles had recently purchased Cobalt's secluded, undeveloped property. Their goal was to escape the confines of the city and commune with nature. Nature, it seemed, was welcome on their new parcel; but snakes were not.

As curator of reptiles at the Mojave Desert Living Museum in the nearby town of Palmdale, I was frequently called to new homesites sprouting up in the once-open desert to remove unwanted pests. To me, it was the new inhabitants, not the old ones, who were unwanted. But be that as it may, I would much rather relocate the snakes than have them destroyed. So whenever the call would come in, I would eagerly respond with snake hook in one hand and a pillowcase in the other. The problem was, with the huge influx of city folk moving to the desert, there were fewer and fewer places left to relocate native wildlife species.

Cobalt was dark black in color with a light gray underside. His home was in the pine forest in what was probably an old badger den. When I approached the snake, he showed no fear of me and absolutely no aggression. There was a brief warning rattle, but even when I coaxed him from his hole with the snake hook, he made no attempt to strike or bite. I gently stuffed him in the pillowcase and tied the top shut securely.

Oh, back to the movie. It was March; and the mountains around Purgatory, Colorado, were not as warm and toasty as the name would imply. I met Charlie, or

Charles Foster Clark, only briefly; and my first impression of him was somewhat shocking. I don't remember ever standing that close to such an immense individual in my life. At nearly seven feet tall and weighing almost three hundred pounds, I wasn't sure how they were ever going to use me, half his size, as a double.

"You don't have any snakes with you, do you?" he asked.

"Well, they're not on me," I answered. "They're in the truck."

"That's a good place for 'em," he said. "I don't much care for snakes." He extended his massive hand and exclaimed, "Pleased to meet ya."

"You're going to catch this rattlesnake with your bare hands?" he asked.

"I will, unless you want to give it a try," I answered.

"Over my dead body," he said. And with that, he turned and walked away.

The following morning, we rehearsed the short snake-capture scene I would be performing. Since most of the focus would be on Cobalt, only my hands and feet would be on film. The "eat the rattlesnake" sequence was actually turkey necks strung together on I-wire. Charlie evidently had no problem with cooking and eating the pretend snakes roasting in the hot coals.

The moment I took Cobalt from his travel bag, everyone but Charlie stepped forward to take a closer look at their first tame rattlesnake. Some of the crew even wanted to pet the snake, and I was happy to oblige.

"Where's Charlie?" I asked one of the crew members.

"Probably somewhere in the next county," he joked. I laid the snake down in the warm sunshine, and he began to crawl instinctually toward the trees. As impressive as he was, there was one part of the shot I wasn't sure Cobalt would be able to perform. An aggressive stance and fierce rattle is what Hollywood expects from a snake. For that shot, I brought along a different rattler, and this one had no trouble showing some attitude. He would be the stunt double for Cobalt, but even I wasn't too excited about wrangling this demon.

In the event of an accident, Cobalt's scenes would be shot first. To my amazement, the man towering in the background watching was no other than Charlie. It appeared as though he had to see it with his own eyes to believe it. It was a little awkward for me to wrangle snakes in this ridiculous outfit, but eventually, I got the hang of it. I had the bright idea that morning that if I placed a bucket over Cobalt, when I yanked it off, he might just stand up and rattle.

The gimmick worked, but by the third take, Cobalt was just too cold to move. Brilliant idea number 2 was in the works. If I slid the frigid snake inside my shirt next to my warm skin, we might be able to get one more shot before changing snakes. There were a few looks of disbelief when I slid Cobalt down inside my clothing, but what happened next threw everyone for a loop. Charlie watched in horror as the large rattlesnake began writhing around trying to get comfortable. In the next minute, the size 13 boots went flying up in the air as Charlie Clark passed out cold.

The poor cowboy just witnessed the worst nightmare he could possibly imagine: a snake crawling around in someone's shirt and worst of all, a rattlesnake!

A medic was called to the set to check on Charlie as we continued shooting Cobalt's final close-up scenes. Everyone helped Charlie into the nearest motor home where he could recover from his panic attack, although all six intelligent men aiding in his rescue failed to read the sign taped securely to the door: WARNING: LIVE RATTLESNAKES INSIDE. The three pillowcases on the bed all contained snakes. And one of them was Cobalt's evil twin. The other two were harmless gopher snakes we picked up in the road on the way to the set.

By the time we learned of Charlie's latest predicament, we were really in a pickle. Those in the crowd who weren't afraid of rattlesnakes were terrified for Charlie. I was elected to peek inside the trailer door and see if the big cowboy was still breathing. If he had the slightest inkling that he was lying on a bed surrounded by snakes, either the snakes would be dead or Charlie would.

I opened the door just wide enough to peek inside. Charlie raised himself up on one arm, allowing me to locate the bags of snakes. The pillowcase closest to his broad head was the one of greatest concern.

"Hey," I said, "are you doing okay?" His complexion was somewhat paler than I remembered, but at least he was breathing.

"You don't have that damn snake in your shirt do you?" he asked.

"No," I answered. "No snakes."

The answer was partially true. The only snakes around were lying dangerously close to a man who was not only as big as a house but was also wearing a gun.

"Hey look, Charlie," I said, edging closer to the bed. "I'm really sorry about the scare I gave you out there."

"Oh," he replied. "I'll recover."

There was a better chance of that really happening if I could figure a way to get that bag relocated without Charlie figuring out what was inside it.

There was a knock at the window on the far side of the room. It was one of Charlie's coworkers peeking in to see if his partner was still kicking. When Charlie rolled onto his left side, I reached up as quietly as I could and ever so gently lifted the snake bag off the bed. Lowering it to the ground, I slid the bag under the bed, calling loudly to the man outside the window in the event that the snake started to rattle. For the time being, Charlie was alive and well; and if I could get the two other bags moved, I would be also. I motioned to the man outside to help me find a way to get Charlie off the bed and out of the trailer. He evidently got the message.

"Charlie, get your lazy ass out here," he said. "That little snake wasn't going to hurt you."

"Don't talk to me about snakes," Charlie replied.

When he rolled over to sit up, his hand was only inches from the other two bags. This could still end all bad.

Thankfully, Charlie Clark managed to right himself without touching the snakes and emerged to a crowd of people clapping their hands in amazement. When he stepped away from the motor home, I made the nearly fatal mistake of closing the door. Looking back, Charlie briefly read the warning sign still taped to the door.

"Not funny," he said, thinking it to be a prank.

"Not funny at all," I said. "Man, I could use a drink."

To this day, I am still uncertain as to whether my snake-fearing friend ever learned the truth about his bunkmates. Just in case the six-shooter hanging on his hip was loaded with more than blanks, I was hoping he never found out.

Cobalt's evil twin played the part of the bad snake exceptionally well and was released as far into the backcountry as I could hike. Why one snake was so gentle and another so vicious, I'll never know. People can be the same.

Cobalt went on to appear in two other movies and numerous school programs. A year later, "he" gave birth to nine baby rattlesnakes. I guess you just can't assume anything! The name was changed to Countess Cobalt, and I spruced up "her" aquarium with a few girly things to make her feel more ladylike. The countess lived in my home for ten more years and died unexpectedly in her sleep. She was always treated with love and respect and would pay it back in kind. There will never be another like her.

Rest in Peace, Countess Cobalt

Hissy Missy

S OME OF THE largest snakes on earth live in regions of Southeast Asia. The reticulated pythons have attained lengths of nearly thirty-three feet and a weight in captivity of two hundred pounds or more.

The rare and deadly faded midget rattlesnake
used in the filming of Man vs Wild with Bear Grillis

Rio; a rescued Redtailed Boa

Missy was not quite so grand a snake in stature but was a beautiful snake nonetheless. A rare Burmese python, Missy was born with a rare genetic deformity. She lacked normal pigment and was therefore an albino.

I first met Missy under unusual and tragic circumstances. She was dying. The year was 1999, and I was attending the first annual camel conference in Cape Girardeau, Missouri. Not a place you would expect to find Burmese pythons, especially snakes measuring over fourteen feet long and white. The gentleman wasn't even speaking directly to me, but I heard the word *snake* and eavesdropped on the conversation.

"It's in that trailer over there," he said. "The guy selling it has been keeping it locked in there for almost a year. Says whoever buys the trailer has to take the snake too. Hell, it looks half-dead to me already, might make a nice pair of boots."

I walked over and peered through the narrow slats. The snake was half-buried in a pile of damp, moldy hay. Her body lay motionless not only from neglect but also from the bitter cold. How she had managed to survive up to this point was a mystery, if she had indeed survived at all.

Not bothering to ask permission, I opened the side door and walked inside. What I found inside was heartbreaking. The snake was barely breathing. Her pale skin hung loosely on her frame, and her breathing was shallow and raspy.

"Who owns this – trailer?" I yelled as I walked out, infuriated by what I had just witnessed. "Does this belong to you?" I demanded, glaring at the man closest to the tailgate.

"No," he barked back. "Check with the gal in the office. And lower your damn voice."

"Sorry," I said, embarrassed by my outburst. "But whoever owns this trailer should be arrested."

"Arrested?" he replied. "Arrested for what?"

I ignored his latest comment and stormed into the office where hopefully I could get some answers. The plump, cheerful woman behind the desk smiled when I walked in.

"Are you here to register for the conference?" she asked.

"I'm already registered," I answered. "Do you know whom that white trailer in the barn belongs to?"

"Is there a problem?" she asked. A look of panic spread across her face.

I realized I probably wasn't going to get a lot of cooperation if I didn't loosen up the attitude, so taking a deep breath, I repeated my question with a little less hostility in my voice.

"Listen," I said, "there's an animal in that trailer that's dying. So before I call the Humane Society and they close this place down, I suggest you find out who owns that 'piece of shit' trailer out there and get him in this office immediately."

"Let me make a phone call, sir. I'm certain we can resolve this without creating a lot of unnecessary hassle. Just give me a minute."

I returned to the trailer to check on the condition of the snake that by now had moved a few inches toward the open door. The small shaft of sunlight streaming in from an open window now shone into the doorway, and the frigid snake was desperately trying to reach its warming rays. The booming voice behind me briefly startled me.

"What's the problem here?" I turned to face the man whose bark appeared to be bigger than his bite.

"Does this trailer belong to you?" I demanded.

"Yeah, it's mine. Who the hell are you?"

His hands were stuffed inside the pockets of the dirty overalls he was wearing. His more-than-ample belly was grotesquely distended over his waist, and by the look on his grimy face, he hadn't washed or shaved for days.

"If this snake dies inside this filthy trailer, I will personally see to it you are prosecuted for cruelty to animals," I yelled back.

A crowd had gathered in the barn, curious about all the commotion.

"Hey, I just bought that trailer. The snake was already in there. The guy who sold it to me said it was a package deal."

A tall gentleman worked his way through the crowd.

"I'm a veterinarian," he said. "Is there a sick animal in there?"

The man in the overalls began to stammer, but I ignored his ramblings and turned my attention to the doctor.

"There's a very skinny python inside this man's horse trailer," I said. "It's barely alive, but if we can get it somewhere warm, we might be able to save it."

"I'm Dr. Murray," the man said, extending his hand. "Let's take the snake in the office and take a look. It's warmer in there, and the lights better."

Dr. Murray was attending the conference as a guest speaker on animal husbandry, and I was delighted he was present on that particular day. I climbed back inside what would soon have become the snake's coffin and kneeled next to her body.

"Careful you don't get bit," Dr. Murray said.

Getting bit was the least of my worries. This poor girl barely had the energy to breathe, let alone bite. We carried the sick snake from the trailer past the bewildered man in the overalls. He just stared down at the ground speechless.

"You should be ashamed," Dr. Murray said. "I'm going to do my best to save this animal, and you, my friend, are going to pay for it."

"Hey, wait a minute. This is, uh – "

That's as far as the objection got when Dr. Murray stopped and looked the man square in the face. "Cruelty to animals is a serious offense, sir, even in the state of Missouri. And I know of at least two people willing to testify against you in court."

"If he will sign the snake over to me," I said, "I'll pay the vet bills if we can try to save her." The man in the overalls nodded in agreement.

"You can have it," he said. "I just wanted the trailer."

By the time Dr. Murray completed his exam on the cold, dehydrated, and half-starved reptile, the man and the trailer had disappeared.

"If this poor animal still has the will to live," Dr. Murray said, "I won't charge you for the treatment. But you'll have to find her a decent home."

"If you can save her," I answered, "she can come home with me."

It was going to be a struggle. If she had survived this long under such horrible conditions, there was the slightest possibility Hissy Missy had the desire to live.

No Pets Allowed

The motel room I booked for the five-day camel conference was nothing to write home about. There was no pool, no weight room, and a breakfast buffet that was the worst I had ever experienced. But I wasn't in Missouri for the cuisine. I was here to learn everything I could about camels and, apparently, rescue a snake.

I emptied the clothes from my duffel bag in order to smuggle Missy into my room. I was fairly certain the sign taped to the door to the lobby, No Pets, probably included Burmese pythons. Dr. Murray's instructions were specific: a warm bath for Missy twice a day and antibiotics every four hours. I filled the tub to the top with as much warm water as I thought she could handle and slowly immersed Missy, tail first. I expected some resistance from my patient, but apparently, a hot bath was just what she was hoping for.

She slipped her head beneath the surface and actually began to drink underwater. Snakes don't lap water as a dog would. They actually suck water as a horse would. For what seemed like an eternity, the snake gulped warm water into her severely dehydrated body until at last, she rose, resurfaced, opened her mouth in a wide yawn, and took a deep breath. The open sores in her mouth presented further testimony to her months of abuse.

Mouth rot is a common but serious condition that can affect reptiles kept in crowded or unsanitary conditions. With proper treatment, the open sores would heal, but the painful abscesses may prevent the python from eating. She still had a long way to go, but I felt Missy was on the road to a slow but steady recovery. Tomorrow when the antibiotics started to kick in, I would feel better about her prognosis. Tonight Missy could relax in a safe, warm shelter where, for once, only her best interests were in mind.

The Flight of Rita Sanchez

EARLY THE NEXT morning, I unzipped Missy's temporary shelter and repeated the bathing and soaking treatment Dr. Murray had recommended. Missy responded in the same manner she had the previous evening by submerging her entire body and taking a long drink. When she repeated her open-mouth yawn, I was able to dab a diluted peroxide solution on her open sores and administer an oral antibiotic treatment. The improvement in her health was subtle, but Missy looked as if she was already beginning to heal.

For every step forward, there is sometimes two steps back; and what transpired next would have little, if any, effect on Missy. It would, though, result in catastrophe for everyone else involved. I would only be gone momentarily. Missy was soaking in the warm bath, allowing me to slip out for a quick bite to eat. I closed the bathroom door in the event the snake decided to explore beyond the confines of the tub and hung the Do Not Disturb sign on the door to avoid any unwelcome intruders into the room. That's where things went astray.

A word to the wise: check both sides of the signs before you hang it on the door. There are two separate and entirely different instructions printed on either side of the placard. They are provided to advise the house cleaning staff as to whether you would like the maid service to clean your room or, in my case, to come back later. I hung my sign backward.

Rita Sanchez hailed from Central America. What inspired her to leave her homeland and end up in Cape Girardeau, Missouri, I will never know. Perhaps Rita came to the States seeking fame and fortune. Maybe she was running away from an abusive husband or poverty or was tired of the perfect weather. Maybe Rita just didn't like snakes. Whatever the reason and due to no fault of her own, Rita's average, boring day was about to take a turn for the worst.

The instructions on the sign were explicit: "Please clean my room promptly" or something to that effect. She entered by knocking first and announcing "house cleaning." When there was no response, she proceeded to tidy up as usual, beginning with, of course, the bathroom.

Now people on vacation have a habit of being a little messy. That's probably why maids wear rubber gloves.

Beds are left unmade, clothing strewn about, and bathrooms, well, they are the worst. Rita had seen it all. Soap, toilet paper, toothpaste, and shaving cream smeared all over everything. Wet, dirty towels scattered all over the floor, socks and underwear hanging on the drying racks. But the last thing Rita ever expected to find lying in the bathtub at her place of employment was a fourteen-foot albino Burmese python with its mouth wide open.

I heard the scream . . . Hell, people in the next county heard the scream! The cleaning cart sailed across the room, and the sound of footsteps fleeing down the stairs and out the door alerted the entire staff that there was a problem in room 204. Those who had a grasp on the Spanish dialect knew what Rita was running from, but they too suspected that Rita was seeing things.

"Monster snake!" she repeated over and over as she fled the building, but no one was able to catch poor Rita for further details.

I arrived back at the room about the same time as the motel manager did, and for the second time in so many days, I was answering the question: "What's the problem here?"

I answered the question openly and honestly, begging leniency. Bob Finlay wasn't biting. I had twenty minutes to pack my belongings and vacate the room or calls would be made. I'm not sure who Bob was going to call, but I wasn't sticking around just in case he was calling Rita's favorite uncle who owned a local gun store or her seven older brothers (I'm guessing on that one) who owned a construction company and also hated snakes.

All's well that ends well, they say. Rita relocated to Hawaii. Snakes are not native to Hawaii and are illegal there. Missy made a full recovery and is living happily in Moab, Utah, with a smaller but equally beautiful boy python.

I was not invited back to the next year's camel conference and have no future plans to vacation in Cape Girardeau, Missouri, although I am certain it has its charm and, for camel lovers, it is a wonderful place to visit.

A Bear Named Casey

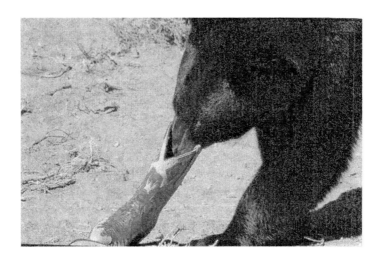

Casey bear retrieving a boot on the movie Back to the Future III

"**T**HEY ARE A dim-witted creature. Today, we are learning specifically about bears," the teacher said. "We will be watching a short film, so pay attention, you will be tested."

It was my senior year in high school, and I was attending my favorite class, zoology. Today's lesson was on mammals.

"There are nine species total," the film's narrator claimed.

It was an old 8 mm. Many years would pass before technology and accurate information on members of the genus *Ursidae* or bears in general would become available. Most of the current data on bears had been conducted on captive animals or the carcasses of trophy bears hunted for their hides and heads. Worse yet, bears worldwide were being slaughtered for their gallbladders. In certain Asian cultures, it was thought that these small organs held some miracle healing properties.

The film went on to show brief clips of the various species of bears in North America: polar bears, brown bears (incorrectly referred to as grizzlies), and of course, the black bears. That is also a misnomer since black bears are not always black but come in a variety of colors. Bears with a cinnamon coloration are sometimes encountered on the temperate rainforests of Washington and Oregon. A brown-colored black bear might occasionally surface in northern California. Then there is the blue-gray-colored bear called glacier bears. These unusually colored animals hunt the rain-drenched forests in Southeast Alaska.

And lastly, there is a very rare yellow or white phase black bear called the Kermode bear. Typically found in British Columbia, the ghost bear is revered in some indigenous cultures. To add even more confusion to the mix, some of the brown bears on Southeast Alaska's Admiralty Island are mostly black while the black bears on a neighboring island are sometimes brown.

Now before you start pulling your hair out, it would also be prudent to mention that the panda bear is classified in its own genus. And koala bears aren't bears at all but marsupials that hail from the continent of Australia.

This all makes sense to me now. As a high school student in the early '70s with barely a 3.0 average, I had little doubt that the effect of mind-altering drugs of the '60s somehow influenced the name classification process used when identifying North American bear species and subspecies throughout the country. With the exception of the polar bear, these animals are omnivores, which is to say they'll eat almost anything. The bulk of a bear's diet is mostly plant matter, so once more, conflict with humans can and will arise.

The sweet smell of an apple pie cooling in the kitchen window or peach trees planted in an open orchard beats the aroma of skunk cabbage in the swamp hands down. Bears are endowed with a sense of smell exceeding even that of a bloodhound and, on occasion, naturally prefer human food with a predictable outcome. Bears and humans locked horns.

Casey's mother was such a bear. Opting to raid the farms surrounding her mountain home in West Virginia, the hungry sow took the unfortunate path of least resistance. After all, she had three cubs to feed. The garbage cans and bowls of dog food were within easy reach, but the human delight was too good to pass up. As the saying goes in West Virginia and elsewhere, "A fed bear is a dead bear."

So by early spring, sadly the sow was shot and the cubs orphaned. A hiker passing by the den heard the desperate cries from the hungry cubs and contacted a local wildlife rescue center. The smallest cub had already succumbed to starvation, and the others were barely able to crawl. At first it was uncertain as to whether the two blind, helpless cubs would survive. But with round-the-clock feedings from a handful of dedicated volunteers, the young bear cubs' survival outlook began to improve.

Now the real challenge began. In order to survive, these cubs would be required to spend their life in captivity. Bear cubs raised by humans could not be returned to the wild. Even if taught how to survive on the plants and animals provided by Mother Nature, their future looked bleak. Their salvation would also be their curse.

Having lost the natural fear of their only predator, man, the young bears would be shot on sight during an upcoming hunting season. Mother bears care for their offspring for the first three years of their life. Their human surrogates would be unable to perform parental duties that would prepare them for their return to the wild. The call went out, but zoos and wildlife parks throughout the country had all the black bears they could handle.

With an estimated one million black bears living in the wilds of North America, a suitable home would be difficult, if not impossible, to find. Even if the young bears were released far from human habitation, their powerful homing instinct would eventually lead them back home. The rapidly developing cubs needed a home soon, and the clock was ticking.

Casey arrived at Cougar Hill Ranch in the first week of May. A hellion from birth, the cub exited his airline crate as a ball of energy. Most young animals had to be coaxed from the safety of a kennel, but Casey was ready to meet the world head on from the moment the door opened.

*   *   *

Nothing is quite as sharp as a suture needle or the claws of an eight-week-old bear cub. Too young to use these sickle-shaped daggers as weapons, Casey's catlike claws served only one purpose, to climb. Trees were the intended target. But the tan hairy legs in front of him were stationary and going in the right direction, skyward. With a short leap, the little bear clawed his way upward into my arms, leaving a trail of tiny bleeding puncture marks from my shin to my thigh.

Typically, there would be a baby bottle full of warm formula at this elevation. Having not eaten since the journey began five hours earlier, Casey Bear, as he would come to be known, was ravenous. The next closest thing to a nipple was attached firmly to the side of my head. My earlobes might not produce milk, but the needle-sharp baby teeth pierced the fleshy appendage, and the hungry cub began suckling with all his might.

In spite of my protests, Casey hung on until, to my relief, a bottle was presented to our newest four-legged family member. He released the beet-red earlobe and reluctantly returned it to its rightful owner. Every heart that day went out to the young orphaned bear cub, and from that day forth, he would become an unforgettable addition to a wildlife oasis that was already full of orphans.

A Cub and a Star

Me as a stunt double for Michael J Fox in Back to the future III

B Y THE TIME Casey reached four months of age, one thing was obvious. The baby bear, born in the lush green hills of West Virginia, was destined to become an actor. Like all juveniles, human and animals alike, Casey was full of mischief and loved to play. If life in the wild wasn't an option for the young cub, then life on the ranch might not be half-bad. There were the loving foster parents and a host of other animals to romp with. But we were not bears.

Wild animals, which are bottle raised by their people parents, develop a strong bond with humans. Casey was no exception. If he wasn't trying to scurry up your pant leg to get eye level, he was trying to topple you over on your back to get you down to his. Visitors to Cougar Hill Ranch were constantly being ambushed by the rapidly growing bear cub, so before long, his free reign on the ranch would need to be curtailed.

Delivery drivers, no longer amused by the antics of the rambunctious young bruin, began leaving their packages at the gate. Other drivers flatly refused to make a delivery at all. In fact, if something on the ranch wasn't being torn down, torn up, or chased around, it was safe to assume Casey was probably sleeping.

Much to his dismay, the little hellion bear cub would need stricter supervision. But since bears can climb out of just about anything that doesn't have the roof bolted down, putting him in a playpen would not be an option either. Housing him in the spacious arena was considered briefly. It was an ideal playground but probably too far from the office. The once-orphaned bear cub would cry pitifully if left alone for more than a minute, so finally a solution was formulated.

Right outside the office door, a steel railroad stake had been hammered into the ground and a steel ring slipped over the head. Attached to the ring was a ten-foot cable secured with a heavy-duty clip. Casey had been fitted with an adjustable nylon dog collar when he arrived on the ranch, so a plan was devised where Casey could be restrained while still in view of a sitter. At first, the self-appointed king of Cougar Hill was not in favor of this new arrangement and would run wildly in circles, bawling out his objections. But in time, the young bear accepted his restricted space and was surrounded by abundant distractions, including a nearby cottonwood tree, to demolish. He settled into his smaller and more controlled existence, but one thing didn't change. Although he was restrained, anyone walking within the twenty-foot diameter of his new domain would still be pounced upon and suffer the wrath of Hurricane Casey.

Eventually, the time came to introduce Casey to what would become a way of life for the young cub. Hollywood was calling, and like a host of other animals on the ranch, Casey was destined to become a star. Born to perform, or so it would appear. We received a call for a short two-day gig with rats. The television movie starred John Voigt and Eric Roberts. The storyboard we received in the mail basically read like this: *escaping from prison through a sewer pipe, the actors would encounter vile rats running along the pipes.*

Easy stuff. The rats were trained to run to a buzzer located at the end of the pipes, and with any luck, we should be able to get the shot in one take. They wouldn't be ready to shoot our scene for a couple hours, so there would be plenty of time to show Casey the inside of a working studio. By introducing animals to the sights, sounds, and smells of a movie set while still young, it becomes a familiar place. When it's their turn to be in front of the camera, life on the set becomes a more positive environment.

Everyone on the set loved the personable little bear, but before long, the entire production came to a halt. While the cast and crew romped with the new celebrity, the director stood by, wringing his hands. Of course, Casey loved the attention, but his presence was costing the company money. Mr. Roberts was particularly smitten with the little cub, and the feeling seemed apparently mutual. To my horror, Casey, as he had done with me, had latched on Eric Roberts's earlobe and began to suckle. The actor was flattered with the bear cub's obvious affection, but failed to realize that removing the amorous youngster from his ear would be no easy feat. The swollen appendage of the human pacifier began to take on the color of overly ripe strawberries, and it was apparent to everyone that something had to be done quickly or Mr. Roberts would soon be sporting a hard-to-explain very visible hickey.

Backing up a few steps for momentum, I rushed forward and grasped the nursing bear by the scruff. In a split second, Casey was wrenched from the earlobe of the startled actor. Casey reacted in a fit of rage by biting down on my arm with needle-sharp teeth while at the same time swinging his equally sharp claws. I was soon bleeding profusely from the numerous puncture marks inflicted by the enraged bear cub, but to my relief, Mr. Roberts was not. In fact, with the exception of the bright-red earlobe, the actor had remained virtually unscathed. At the conclusion of the day's shoot, we were invited back the following day to complete a couple pickup shots. But unfortunately, Casey, the suckling bear cub from hell, was not.

Casey Goes Hollywood

BY HIS THIRD summer, Casey, although still gangly, had developed a powerful chest and strong forearms. His training was going well, and the young bear could quickly learn a new behavior when properly motivated. For me, life on the ranch was the best it had ever been. I rented a small trailer in a mobile home park a quarter mile up the road, and by first light, I was usually ready to start the day.

Although Casey was still technically a cub, he had matured considerably, and the destructive characteristics he exhibited earlier in his life began to diminish. He now revealed a calmer, more controlled demeanor. There was one aspect of his personality however that would remain constant. Next to eating, the one thing the young bear loved to do was wrestle.

After a hearty breakfast of fresh fruit, veggies, and boiled chicken, the well-rested bear would rise up on his back legs and, lowering his head, prepare to do battle. His pattern was usually predictable – grab his opponent behind the knees, and with a sweeping motion, push headlong into the combatant's stomach, upending the challenger. The secret to bear wrestling was never to let Casey get you on the ground. If you could remain upright, you had a fighting chance. But once the bear toppled you over, you lost the match and usually had to call in reinforcements to regain your stance and continue the bout.

In nature, play fighting would prepare a young bear for the challenges he would face as an adult, which included defending his territory, finding a mate, and avoiding predators. These were all part of surviving in the wild. But in captivity, he would not encounter these obstacles, so wrestling became more of a favorite pastime. As Casey grew, his skill level increased to the point that, for me, winning the round was no longer an option. But running was.

"If you can't beat 'em, get the hell out of there," I'd always say. His small baby teeth were soon replaced with large powerful canines, teeth that were capable of ripping and tearing flesh. But Casey, even in the heat of mock battle, was careful not to inflict serious injury on his opponent. That is until one fateful day when I was reminded that the once-playful cub, although trained, was now grown and inherently still a wild animal.

There is a bestselling novel that was an easy read, and its popularity in the elementary schools throughout the country eventually led to the movie version. *Hatchet* was the story of a young boy stranded in the Canadian wilderness after the pilot flying him across the mountains suffered a heart attack and died. The plane went down in an alpine lake, but surviving the crash was just part of the ordeal. The young lad was now faced with the daunting task of staying alive with nothing more than a hatchet.

A resident black bear, portrayed in the movie version by Casey, helped teach the boy the skills he would need in order to survive the hostile new environment. As with all well-written movies, there was one catch. The human posed a possible threat to the bear's new cubs and, in the process of attempting to drive the intruder off, attacked and mauled the boy in the lake.

I was somewhat taller than the young actor Jared Rushton who starred in the film, but with a wig and a matching outfit, we were able to pull it off. The drive to the pristine lake in northern California was about ten or twelve hours, so by the time we arrived, the sun was just beginning to set. We checked in to the small motel on the outskirts of town. While Nick's sister, Liz and I set about feeding and watering the animals, Nick parked and leveled the modified horse trailer.

In addition to Casey, we also brought along the other animal actors that would appear in the film. Suki, the white wolf, had several scenes; and Bandit, a young male raccoon, had his part. There were two young bear cubs that portrayed Casey's cubs, and last but not least, there was the cantankerous old porcupine that made a habit of showing up uninvited and leaving his calling card – a leg full of quills of the stranded, frightened castaway.

The first week of shooting was mostly about Jared – looking for food, building a shelter, and learning to make fire. Nothing was filmed in the same order as the movie was written. The animal scenes were mostly uneventful, but anytime the script called for a close interaction between the human actor and the animals, I was called in for the double.

In the old days, the actors themselves did many of their own stunts. Falling off horses, jumping off roofs, or being attacked by a pack of Rottweilers was all part of the job. Now it's the stuntman or the double who takes all the risk. But it's also the most fun and exciting.

The night shoot with the raccoon was a bit of a fiasco. Bandit was supposed to enter the small shelter the boy built using his trusty axe and wander around the cave looking for food. All went well until he detected the faint scent of dog food that I had inadvertently left in my rear pocket. I was positioned face up in the recumbent position, trying to act as if I were sound asleep. The little varmint couldn't roll me over, so he did the next best thing. Sticking his nose as far up my crotch as he could reach, Bandit began to burrow his way in. The only possible way I was going to be able to keep from laughing was either being dead or numb from the waist down. By the third or fourth take, I was able to remain motionless just long enough to get the shot.

Finally, the day arrived for the bear attack sequence. Casey was put on a long leash in the shade while we went over the shot. Once more, I would be running from the king of wrestling. But this time, there was an added incentive. The handful of apple slices in my shirt pocket was temptation enough. But the chance to dunk me in the lake was all the motivation the frisky bear needed. Then all hell broke loose.

Always sticking his nose where it doesn't belong, curious Casey dug up a hornet nest. While trying to escape the angry bees, Casey was bawling at the top of his lungs, and that left him in a real bind. The heavy metal chain was holding fast, and try as he might, the poor bear could not escape his tormentors. Nick was first on the scene, and in spite of his allergy to bee stings, he waded into the stand of trees and untied the frightened bear. The bear bolted from the trees like he was on fire. Now a bear is pretty thick-skinned, so the only place the angry wasps could connect was on the tips of the ears and the end of his nose. Assuming he was all right, we continued with the shot. That decision would be one that I would come to regret.

Still angry from his encounter with the hive, Casey followed me into the lake at a full run. Raising his upper body from the water, he wrapped both paws around my neck in a viselike grip. I knew by the intensity in which he was wrestling that something was wrong. A solid blow to the right side of my head sent the wig flying down the front of my face. I pushed the agitated bear back with all my might, but in the process made contact with the still-tender nose.

Bear-attack victims say the only way you can tell when a bear is really angry and not bluffing is when the whites of their eyes turn red. Looking at Casey eye to eye, I knew I was in trouble.

"Back up," I shouted, hoping to intimidate the bear into backing down.

Gripping me even more, he raised his paw for another blow; but by this time, I had had enough. A cuff to the chin followed by a right hook to the nose was usually enough to let Casey know I was serious. I thought it worked when he backed up a step or two. But then, as if in slow motion, Casey lashed out with his deadly canines.

Fortunately, he came back to his senses and, realizing he had just committed the inexcusable act, released my arm from his powerful jaws. Casey turned back toward the shore, and with water flying in all directions, he headed toward Nick and Liz. Totally unaware that my arm had just been ripped open, the camera continued to roll.

"That looked great," the director said as I walked from the water, looking down at my exposed tendons and veins. Casey was standing behind Liz, peering out from behind her body. To my surprise, there was virtually no pain. Or to be more specific, there was no pain yet.

"Got it in you to do another take?" Nick asked.

"I think I'm going to need a few stitches first," I replied. I showed him the nasty four-inch wound on my arm, and he looked stunned.

"Casey bit you?" he asked. But Nick already knew the answer to the question.

"We need to get this man to a hospital," he shouted.

Everyone looked in our direction, thinking we were pulling their leg. But the ashen color of my skin and the blood streaming down my arm assured them that I was not.

Casey's Revenge

THE CELL PHONES of yesterday are nothing like the complicated devices we see today. The earlier models were carried in a small suitcase, and the batteries alone were four times the size of the compact wafer-thin phones commonly seen now. These old phones were often unreliable and cumbersome at best, but on this particular day, it would come in handy if we could only get it to work.

The emergency phone call to the local hospital in Shasta County, California, got the attention of the entire medical staff. The receptionist could barely decipher the garbled, frantic voice on the other line but was able to make out two words clearly: BEAR ATTACK!

The transportation captain loaded me into his pickup truck. He wrapped my arm in a gauze bandage from the first aid kit and began the forty-five-minute drive to town. The pain was beginning to set in, but for now it was bearable (no pun intended). Nick and Liz put Casey Bear back in the trailer to calm him down, and the production company began setting up for another shot.

The ride to town on the gravel road was slow and bumpy. The driver and I had a casual relaxed conversation, mostly about training animals. He raised Labs, and the enthusiasm in his voice told me these dogs were his babies. He talked about their different personalities and impressed me with his dedication to his pets. Although he had no formal training, his techniques overall were sound. The conversation made the time go by quickly, and before long, we were pulling up to the entrance of the emergency room. When we arrived, I walked to the front counter while Raft, the driver, parked the truck. By this time, the bleeding had stopped; so besides the dull ache and tingling sensation in my fingertips, I was in a pretty good shape.

Up to this point, I was unaware of the fact that the hospital had received the garbled phone call of an alleged bear attack. Therefore, I had no idea a welcoming committee would be awaiting our arrival. All eyes were entranced on the emergency room door. There hadn't been a bear attack in the small town since the '50s; and everyone, except the mayor, had been called in to witness the gruesome carnage.

I was immediately dismissed due to the fact that I was ambulatory and my head was firmly attached to my shoulders. By all outward appearances, I was probably some tourist who sprained his wrist playing tennis. I remained at the front counter as the pleasant elderly receptionist politely asked, "How can I help you?" She never actually made eye contact with me but instead passed a clipboard in my direction.

Something tragic had obviously occurred here, I thought, and my insignificant injuries were the least of her worries. Perhaps the local school bus had been involved in an accident or a passing train had derailed, scattering passengers along the rails. Whatever calamity had occurred, the entire hospital staff had been put on full alert.

"I need to get some stitches," I replied, keeping my eyes on the door.

"What's going on?" Raft asked as he walked in and looked around like he had just entered the twilight zone.

"Somebody up at the lake got mauled by a bear," the receptionist replied, looking briefly in Raft's direction.

Still unaware a call had been made, I was temporarily shocked by the statement. Black bears rarely attack humans and . . . I stopped there. It suddenly dawned on me everyone was waiting for a camper or hiker who had been attacked by a wild bear. No one had informed them the attack was by a trained bear on a movie set. Without thinking about the possible consequences of his statement, Raft blurted out, "He got attacked," pointing to me.

Before long, I was surrounded by the entire special victims unit of Podunk, California, all firing out questions simultaneously. This was more excitement than this little ER had seen since the alien abduction back in 1974 when a local farmer found his sixteen-year-old daughter wandering in circles in the cornfield muttering.

"They were all green!" someone proclaimed.

The girl was escorted by the sheriff to the hospital, and it was determined the green she was referring to was not actually little green men as suspected but little green mushrooms sprouting from the cow patties out in the pasture. Ingested with the poor girl as a scientific experiment of sorts, the riddle was solved when the unpalatable green fungi were disgorged onto the new boots of the attending physician.

One step ahead of Casey Back to the Future III

"Where were you attacked?" one man asked me.

"Fisher Lake," I replied.

"Where was the bear?" someone else inquired.

"Same lake," I answered.

"What were you doing in a lake with a bear?"

"We were wrestling," I said, frustrated with all the questions.

"Wrestling?" everyone said in unison.

It was quite apparent by this time that the crucial details about the injuries inflicted by the bee-stung bear had been omitted on the phone call to the emergency room staff.

"Hold up," I said, raising my one good arm in the air. "Nobody was mauled by a bear."

A disappointing groan erupted in the room, and the crowd began to disperse, though a few curious spectators stayed behind to hear about what had actually happened. As the doctor removed the dressing from my painful arm, I replayed the story to the remainder of onlookers. Most of which were too bored or too lazy to move on. We arrived back on the set by early afternoon, and the director instructed the crew that we were losing light. Apparently, he was anxious to finish the bear attack scene before dark.

Casey had pretty much calmed down; so against doctor's orders, I ran back into the cold lake, wig and all, to finish up on a most unforgettable day. The movie, *A Cry in the Wild*, was a big hit for the fans. Based on the book *Hatchet*.

Casey went on to appear in numerous other films and commercials. With his famous trained snarl and natural love for mischief, Casey was always a huge hit, but it was the bear's personality that made him a natural. In the movie *Back to the Future III*, Casey preformed one of his most memorable stunts.

I would double Michael J. Fox in the cave scene, which was filmed in Monument Valley, Arizona. Casey played a bear annoyed by the intrusion of having a DeLorean being parked in his den, so he chases the intruder into the desert where he tumbles down a hill and is knocked unconscious.

While appearing in his starring role as Baloo in the live-animal version of *Jungle Book*, Casey once more displayed his true talent as an animal actor. Casey retired from his acting career after twenty-five years. Although he has slowed down considerably from his younger days, there is always just enough spunk, even now, for a good wrestling match.

In 1995, I headed back to Alaska to explore a new adventure that included living with brown bears for two seasons in a remote wilderness valley called Redoubt Bay. There I would come to find out that whatever I thought I knew about bears from reading books or bottle raising orphaned cubs was miniscule compared to what I was about to discover. That summer I would come face-to-face with North America's largest and possibly least understood carnivore.

Ursus Horribilis
The Horrible Bear

My new home was located on a remote glacial-fed lake and was an hour's flight by bush plane from Anchorage. Originally built as a hunting camp, the new owners, Carl and Kirstin Dixon, hoped to preserve the few remaining bears at Redoubt Bay as a living attraction for future generation of Alaskan visitors.

It was still spring when I arrived at the small cabin nestled on a small knoll in the spruce trees. The plane touched down on the still partially frozen water, being careful to avoid the large patches of ice that could easily puncture the floats. We quickly unloaded the month's worth of supplies I would need to get by until the next supply plane arrived.

It would be a big job refinishing the neglected two-room cabin in order to house any guests we may attract in the upcoming summer season. The pilot departed after a firm handshake and advised me to keep the doors locked whether I was there or not.

"If the bears get in, they'll eat you out of house and home," he warned.

Thanking him for the advice, I watched him circle the cabin once. Then tipping his wings in a final goodbye, he disappeared into the west. Once the drone of the aircraft faded into the distance, I stood on the small porch of the drafty cabin. This was, without a doubt, one of the quietest places on earth. In a couple of months, the migrating sockeye and coho salmon would begin their migration back to the place of their birth, and the brownies, hungry from the long winter hibernation, would once more converge on the fish-rich steams feeding into the bay. This time, however, they would not be pursued by hunters looking for another wall mount, though the bears of Redoubt Bay would be protected and preserved. I would eventually bet my life on it.

Jinda Meets the Bears

Mother Brown Bear with cubs Diver and Wee Bear

THE DREAM OF living in the Alaskan wilderness had once more come true. The cabin would need some work, but the scenery was breathtaking. Black Peak loomed in the background at fourteen thousand feet in elevation. Covered in glacial ice, this jagged pinnacle was the gateway to the vast, untamed Lake Clark Wilderness.

The only sound I awoke to was that of ice cracking on the frozen lake and the haunting cry of a Northern loon. Soon a variety of other waterfowl would follow the loon to this avian paradise. Trumpeter swans, Canada geese, and green-winged teal all made Redoubt Bay their summer home. Countless other birds also lived on and around the lake during the brief summer season. Food for the birds was plentiful here as were the predators who anxiously awaited their arrival.

Tracks in the snowbank alongside the cabin were unmistakable. A red fox digging for holes had passed by in the early-morning hours. Small droplets of blood were still present, suggesting her hunt had been successful. Webbed feet and a slide on the muddy banks of the lake showed evidence that river otters also resided here. The white-fronted goose, an endangered species in Alaska, gave this region its status as a protected habitat. The mating birds would need to pay heed if they chose to nest here. An entire clutch of eggs could be lost in an instant to a hungry family of otters. Many of the young goslings would perish by summer's end, but all of this is part of the ebb and flow of life in the Alaska wilderness.

New life would be forthcoming on the lake, but not any time soon. Winter had not yet released her icy grip on the land, and the frost on the cabin windows tempted me to remain beneath the pile of warm comforters. At last, I arose to greet the dawn and begin my new adventure here. Fire was the first order of the day. A few coals still glowing from the previous night would make the job easier. The small wood stove was an insufficient heat source for the crudely built cabin. The gaps in between the log walls instantly sucked the warm air from the small living space and replaced it with a bitter cold. Socks, old newspapers, and mud had been stuffed into the cracks to keep out the cold; but this small structure had been built primarily as a summer shelter. For the next few years, this would be my year-round home; and in order to survive here, the cabin would require a more permanent type of insulation. After breakfast, I decided to begin the task.

The warming rays of the sun began to appear on the horizon. The exterior walls of the weathered cabin appeared sound, but the burrowing tracks of beetle larvae indicated that life-forms arrive soon. It had been this way since the beginning of time.

Short-faced bears, the ancestors of the brown bears, haunted these mountains and valleys eons ago. Survival then, like now, would depend on the migrating sockeye; but there was one drastic element that threatened the survival of this once unchallenged monarch. A new, mightier predator had emerged. Mankind with its superior weaponry could slay the animals by land and by air. The hunter had become the hunted, and the lives of the mighty Alaskan brown bear would be changed forever. A plane laden with supplies arrived from Anchorage on the first week of July. The salmon were working their way up the river at last, and final preparations were underway to ready the cabin for any arriving guests.

The two-man floatplane landed safely on the lake and taxied to the dock. A very important passenger would be on board today. The moment the cargo door opened, she bound out of the plane. With tail wagging, Jinda dashed up the trail and jumped in my arms. My best friend and fellow adventurer had arrived at last.

Jinda, an Australian cattle dog with a little husky thrown in, was born in Southeast Alaska two years ago. A friend and I picked her out of a litter of six puppies. From birth, Jinda was fearless and loyal to a fault. No human could match the dedication this wonderful canine had shown me from the very beginning of her young life. I had hoped she could join me when I first arrived here, but her duties lay elsewhere in Juneau, so I waited patiently for her arrival. Circling the cabin and the surrounding forest, the young heeler instantly became aware of every living thing that had passed by recently. A red squirrel scampered up a tree, tail swishing furiously. Jinda had one major obsession in life. All squirrels belonged up in the trees, and her goal in life was to make sure that they remained there.

More important than that, Jinda would always place my safety before that of her own and rushed to intercept any perceived danger. Willing to risk her very life to protect me was her self-appointed duty. It was that quality and her superb senses that would eventually rescue me at Redoubt Bay Lodge on more than one occasion.

The first bear we would encounter at the cabin was not the brown bears I had come here to observe. Otis, as he came to be known, was a male black bear. At perhaps two hundred pounds or so in weight, Otis was a sizable yet surprisingly timid brute.

At last, the warming rays of the sun began to appear on the horizon. The exterior walls of the weathered cabin appeared sound, but the burrowing tracks of beetle larvae indicated that life forms flourished beneath the thick bark. It looked as though everything that existed here was part of a never ending food chain. That food chain apparently included my new home. Large claws mark above the front door stopped me in my tracks. Reaching nearly ten feet high, this was no Black Bear.

A resident brownie had laid claim to this small plot of land, and the deep gouges in the log wall was a warning to any other bears that this was his turf. I knew that the Alaskan brown bear could stand over ten feet tall and weigh up to a thousand pounds. It was highly unlikely that the flimsy cabin door would be capable of keeping a hungry, or territorial bear of this size out. After caulking the log walls, I would begin constructing a new bear-proof door.

Time passed quickly, and by early June, the cabin was at last ready. New cupboards were erected in the makeshift kitchen area. Four bunks were built from two-by-fours and plywood and were assembled in the loft. Guests would be arriving soon to witness a great spectacle: the annual migration of thousands of sockeye salmon. With the salmon, though, came the predators, both bird and beast, predators that feasted on the protein-rich fish.

Bald eagles were the first to appear. Cruising on the warm thermals, the great birds scoured the winding river flowing to the ocean only nine miles away. For now, the great bears remained in the high country meadows, feeding on new shoots, sedges, and the occasional hoary marmot. The groundhog-sized rodents were wary, but any marmot foolish enough to stray from the safety of their boulder-strewn burrow would quickly be captured and devoured.

Moose and caribou with newborn calves in tow also entered these clearings to feast on the summer grasses and flowers. The snow-white Dall sheep stayed close to the steep cliffs, relying on the protection afforded by the precarious ledges. The wild sheep were quick to flee in order to safeguard their newborn lambs if the hungry bears venture too close.

Many young ungulates would perish in these meadows in order to satiate the appetite of the hungry bruins. Anything edible could and would be devoured as the bears sought to replace fat reserves lost during hibernation. The sows were particularly famished after a long winter's sleep and would feed round the clock. With ravenous cubs by their side, they began working their way down to the creeks. Instinctually they knew the migrating and life-sustaining salmon would arrive soon. It has been this way since the beginning of time.

Jinda as always was walking ahead of me on the narrow dirt trail. I was changing the oil on the diesel-powered generator. Engrossed in the task at hand, I was not paying much attention to what lay ahead. Stopping abruptly, the fearless dog with hackles raised let out a deep growl, certain we had stumbled onto a dangerous brown bear, possibly even a mother bear with cubs. I began to back up slowly while removing the pepper spray canister from the holster on my belt.

"Jinda, come!" I said. I was hoping my once-well-trained dog would follow my command and retreat.

At the sound of my voice, the startled bear feasting on blueberries rose to its hind legs to get a better fix on the intruders who had interrupted its breakfast. Letting out a loud woof, the bear began popping its jaws. Jaw popping was an intimidation technique that would send most dogs running; but Jinda, sensing my life was in danger, emitted a fierce bark and launched an attack on the startled bear.

Any encounters Otis previously had with dogs would certainly pale by comparison to the forty-pound demonic bundle of ferocity that confronted the poor beast now. Being a heeler, Jinda circled behind the quarry, snapping at his heels. Before Otis could turn to protect his flank, the lightning-fast dog disappeared in the tall grass only to reappear nipping and snapping at the poor animal again.

By this time, Otis was just looking for a safe exit. A nearby spruce tree might suffice, so dashing forward, the frustrated bear leaped up the sturdy tree trunk only to find the pesky tormentor attached to its rump.

"Leave it!" I shouted.

But by this time, the aggressive little cow dog was not yet willing to give up the fight. Otis, in a futile attempt to rid himself of the aggressive pest, reached back to swat at Jinda who at last declared victory and released her grip on the angry bear.

Otis spent the better part of the day in the safety of the tree while Jinda and I returned to the cabin. By late afternoon, he finally dropped to the ground and disappeared hastily into the forest. Otis would be a frequent visitor to the lodge, and Jinda eventually became somewhat used to his occasional presence. But an invisible boundary was established between the two animals, and if the bear stayed a respectable distance from both me and the cabin, a peaceful truce was possible. On the few occasions the trespassing bear crossed the line however, the fierce little dog gave chase to the retreating interloper, reminding him of the acceptable bear-dog etiquette.

One summer morning when a brown bear ventured across the lake, Jinda showed considerable restraint. She still drove the bear from the property, keeping a respectable distance from the brownie. By allowing the more sullen brown bear a chance to depart the premises and still retain its dignity, the two animals could call it a draw. Guests at the lodge loved the little cattle dog, and year after year, I would receive letters and e-mails inquiring about Jinda.

Of the countless visitors to visit Redoubt Bay, one would be a most memorable character. The tale of this fly-fishing wonder woman would forever go down in history as the single most insane fishing story ever told. Jinda, of course, would be on hand to save the day.

It was an unusually quiet morning at the lodge, and the two guests staying with us had decided to sleep in. The sound of a floatplane landing and then departing a short time later sparked my curiosity. Jinda accompanied me across the lake to investigate. It would be a lifesaving decision that we would make on that fateful day, and I often wondered what the outcome might have been had we not made the trip.

Wolverine Creek was only half a mile from the property. As the name would imply, the cold, clear creek emptied into the lake from a series of higher lakes, the first being Wolverine Lake. Legend has it that a wolverine attacked and killed a trapper here sometime around the turn of the century. The story was suspicious at best, and it was most likely one of many fables created by an early explorer to the region.

It is quite possible that the ill-fated trapper was robbed of his furs, and the culprit fabricated the entire story to cover up his crime. In any event, thousands of sockeye salmon would congregate at the mouth of Wolverine Creek, which attracted a host of two-legged as well as four-legged fishermen. In this case, it was a fisherwoman dressed up in her full outdoor attire. The middle-aged woman looked like a poster child for an L.L. Bean catalog. It was uncommon to find people fishing without the safety of a floatplane. The territorial bears could be present at the creek on any given day. Most kept a respectable distance from one another, so conflict between bears and fishermen was rare. Some of the locals carried a sidearm to warn off any of the bears that approached too closely. Most of the gun touting was for show and the wannabe bushmen pretending to be cowboys on the Last Frontier.

On this particular morning, there were no bears to be found, and there was only one fisherman. The young woman seemed annoyed by our intrusion and was apparently in no mood for conversation. She was perched atop a large flat boulder at the mouth of the inlet. The water was teeming with salmon waiting to make a dash up the shallow creek to their spawning beds in Wolverine Lake. Now don't get me wrong, no one likes their quiet time in the wilderness more than I do, but the problem as I saw it was the rock.

You see, that flat boulder was the private property of Diver. Diver, you may wonder, was a two-year-old brown bear cub that accompanied his mother and two siblings, Dagger and Wee Bear, to the lake every morning to fish. I gave Diver his name due to his unorthodox method of fishing. Diving in the water in pursuit of the salmon rather than waiting for the fish to swim up the shallow stream. Most bears preferred to stream fish because they were easier to catch.

Diver's favorite launching spot was none other than the exact same boulder presently occupied by the fisherman. Exactly what reaction Diver may or may not have to this two-legged intruder for trespassing on his rock was unknown. What is known, however, is getting too close to a Mama Bear and her cubs is really bad news. So I hoped to politely intervene.

"Where did your plane go?" I inquired, trying not to sound too demeaning.

"Back to town, I assume," the lady replied.

The irritation at my questioning was quite apparent in her voice. Pilots knew better than to leave fishermen unattended in bear country. The outcome could be fatal for both fisherman and bears, but something told me that this woman was not used to being told no. So the pilot, against his better judgment, had left the woman to her own resources. She was about to discover the perils of fly-fishing in Alaska the hard way.

"All that poop on the hillside behind you doesn't belong to dairy cows," I said. I was slightly annoyed at her apparent lack of good judgment.

"I'll be fine," she snapped back.

"You'll be fine all right," I told her. "That is, until Diver gets here."

I also considered leaving the woman to what would certainly end in disaster, but just about then, Jinda smelled the family of bears before either of us was aware of their approach. The hackles on her neck became erect, and the growl in her throat was telling me the bears were close by. I moved the boat forward to retrieve the stubborn fisherman from her precarious perch, but Diver arrived to the rock before I did.

Thinking back, the look of abstract horror on the woman's gaunt face was almost comical. Glancing behind her at an entire family of brown bears with Diver in the lead definitely got her attention. Converging on the large, flat boulder where the woman was trapped, the bears paused momentarily to ponder this dilemma. The prospect of becoming bear chow soon resulted in all color draining from the fisherman's face. But rather than slide down off the rock into the safety of the boat, she opted to leap headlong into the lake.

A pair of hip waders filled with lake water does not make a great flotation device. It is a great way to sink directly to the bottom. Before she went under a second time, I reached the frantic woman, possibly preventing her from embarking on her final voyage to the salmon-spawning grounds at the bottom of the lake.

"I told you so" wasn't really prudent at that particular moment, so I dragged her waders and all into the boat. As expected, everything that happened in this person's life was everyone else's fault. As she sat shivering by the woodstove, awaiting a flight back to town, I fixed her a cup of hot tea, attempting to strike up a conversation; but she just sat.

When the pilot finally arrived, I had to ask, "Why would you leave a single fisherman alone on a creek filled with bears?"

"Did you try talking any sense into that woman?" he asked me.

"Several times," I answered.

"Well then, you already know the answer." There was a look of exasperation on his face, so we dropped the conversation.

Indeed, true to form, she departed without a single gesture of appreciation or word escaping from her shivering blue lips.

Some people, I thought, really get the most out of a wilderness fishing trip to Alaska. I am sure she was one of those people.

The Rescue of Diver

THERE WOULD BE countless exciting and memorable experiences I would enjoy while living at the bear lodge on Redoubt Bay. Indeed, an entire book could be written on the subject, but I would like to share one final story of my life there with my wonderful dog, Jinda. Over one summer, I had more exciting adventures there than at any time in my life.

There was, of course, an occasional tragic death of a bear at Wolverine Creek. Numerous mother bears would bring their cubs to the fishing hole to learn the fine art of catching salmon. Some were newborns, but others I would have the pleasure of watching grow into subadults. Each one had its own unique personality. Some were shy, others bold, dominant, playful, or adventurous.

A few of the bear cubs would unexpectedly just disappear. One reason for the missing cubs was predation by male bears. A sow cares for her young for the first three years. During that time, she is unavailable for breeding with the amorous males. If by chance she loses her youngsters, the female bear typically comes back into season. Although a mother bear will fight to the death to protect her young, a boar kills and eats a certain number of bear cubs annually.

In the fall of '97, I would meet such a predatory bear, and it would be one of the most chilling encounters I would ever experience. I was fishing with a young couple from Germany at Wolverine Creek that day. It had been cold and rainy for the better part of the week, and we were about to call it a day when the big boar emerged from the trees.

Several adult female bears and their cubs were dining on salmon at the fishing hole. Other bears were waiting for the salmon in the lake to make another run. Diver, as usual, was swimming and wrestling with his sister in the water directly in front of the boat. A four-year-old male bear was also present. He was a frequent visitor to the lodge when the larger bears chased him away from the creek. We called him Gypsy due to an unfortunate incident at Wolverine Creek. Gypsy discovered and consequently rolled on an open tackle box left carelessly on the bank. The old fishing lures lodged in his fur, and one hook lodged in his lip.

The bear looked as though he was sporting a new array of costume jewelry, and it reminded me of a gypsy. The name, like the rusty fishhooks, just stuck. Beautea, the female angler on my boat, alerted us to the fact that a bear fight was going on far upstream. The loud roaring, accompanied by breaking branches, indicated that the fight was heading our way.

The sows began gathering up their cubs and moved away from the oncoming ruckus. The frightened bear could be seen running down the creek at full speed. When he burst through the trees, I could tell it was Gypsy. The large gash on his rear flank indicated he was possibly losing the fight. A moment later, I could understand why. The contender was immense. In fact, it was the largest wild bear I had ever seen. Immediately, I pulled up the anchor and began moving into deeper water. The new beach master stopped his pursuit of Gypsy and began to survey the small cove for another target. By now most of the bears had disappeared into the thick underbrush, but in all the excitement, Diver and Wee Bear became trapped in the lake.

The scarred muzzle on the huge boar suggested he was a killer. This bear had evidently fought many a battle, and his next meal was only a few yards away. Fortunately for him, Mama Bear was nowhere to be seen. The rules are simple. Whatever happens in nature is fate. For humans to intervene, frankly, is against the rules of nature; but this was Diver. To just stand by while the big boar killed him would be unbearable for me. We all began to shout at once. I was slapping the water with the oars of the boat, hoping to scare the hungry male bear away from the helpless cubs.

The distraction, however, wasn't working; and the predacious bear began moving in the direction of the two very frightened cubs. If you ever watched a movie where the hero suddenly appears out of nowhere and rescues the damsel in distress, that's pretty much how this all played out. Mama Bear, realizing she was missing a couple of her cubs, plowed her way through the alder trees and charged headlong at the big boar that was threatening her cubs. We were like a bunch of armchair quarterbacks shouting out the next move.

"Get him! Bite his head off! Kill that – ."

The scarred-up old male had enough. Even though he towered over the smaller female bear, the risks involved were too great. Both bears were standing on their hind legs, feigning an attack. The sparring went on for several more seconds and the noise was deafening, but eventually, the huge boar began to back away. Mama Bear continued to back him farther from the cubs until, at last, the two combatants dropped back to all fours. With jaws still popping, they moved in separate directions.

I am uncertain what affect, if any, we had in the rescue of Diver and his sister. But when it was over, we all breathed a sigh of relief. Survival for all the bears at Redoubt

Bay was crucial. Even the scarred up old boar, that one we named PacMan, had the right to survive. In nature, it's kill or be killed; so if Diver and the other cubs were ever to survive to adult hood, they too would have to learn the hard lesson Gypsy was taught that day. I vowed to never again interrupt the wild bears at Redoubt Bay. I only hoped that next time it wouldn't be Diver.

A Night with the PacMan

TO DISCOURAGE THE bears from associating our cabins as a food source, all food waste was stored in a small log shed behind the house. Whenever supplies were delivered via floatplane, the pilot would haul the trash back to Anchorage on his return trip. Bears have a tremendous sense of smell, so occasionally, Otis or Gypsy would show up at night and try his luck at breaking into the garbage shed. Jinda, sleeping at the foot of the bed, would alert me with a low, deep growl whenever the prowlers showed up. This was typically followed by a single bark that would wake me from my sleep. By banging a couple of pans conveniently left hanging by the two-foot-by-three-foot open window, I could usually send the intruder on its way.

Less than a week after the attack on Gypsy, I was awakened by my canine bear alarm. This time, however, something was different. Jinda's growl was not followed by a bark but a worried whine.

"Where's the bear?" I asked her. She looked anxiously at the window but remained near the bed. I was still half-asleep, but something told me not to be too hasty. Snatching the soup pans from the hook near the window, I whipped open the delicate curtains and prepared to give the pesky bear a good scare. But this time, the surprise was on me.

Less than a yard away, a head the size of a Volkswagen swung in my direction, and the chestnut brown eyes focused on my own. The scarred muzzle of massive size instantly identified this animal as the one bear living at Redoubt Bay I had hoped to avoid. One of the large upper canine teeth was broken, and the ears were tattered and torn. I could smell the bear's rancid breath lingering in the air and knew I should back away from the window. But for whatever reason, my legs refused to listen to my brain. For what felt like an hour, I remained frozen in place, gawking at the biggest, scariest brown bear I had ever imagined. Jinda's frightened growl startled me from my trance, and I stumbled back from the window, tripping over my boots in the process. For a moment, I thought about the new door I had built to keep the bears outside. Nothing, I thought, would keep this brute out should he decide to smash his way into the cabin.

For a moment, I considered I might be dreaming. I looked around the bedroom, and the alarmed look on my little cattle dog's face assured me this was no dream. Quietly I made my way into the living room to block the front door with whatever I could find, but the sight of long, shaggy silhouette of the bear in the kitchen window caused me to stop in my tracks. As the immense bear circled the cabin, his huge frame filled the picture widow. I stood looking out over the lake while Jinda sat by the door, sniffing at the small gap near the floor. Every hair on her body was standing erect. I could hear the sound of the four-inch bear claws raking across the wooden porch.

"What's going on?" The voice startled me. I certainly didn't need any more of an adrenaline rush than I was already having. The young couple from Germany sleeping in the loft was awakened by the commotion.

"Is somebody here?" Yeargan asked.

"It's PacMan," I answered.

"PacMan?" he repeated.

"The big boar we saw at Wolverine Creek a couple of days ago," I said. "He's on the porch." I crammed a sturdy kitchen chair under the doorknob.

"Can he get in?" Yeargan asked with a distinct sound of fear in his quivering voice.

"I don't think so," I replied. "But just in case, Jinda and I better sleep in the loft with you two."

I lifted my reluctant dog up the ladder and grabbed a comforter and pillow from the bedroom then climbed the rickety ladder into the loft. We got little sleep that night as we listened to PacMan wander around outside the cabin. It seemed like an eternity; but in the wee hours of the morning, silence once more enveloped the lodge, and we drifted off to sleep.

No one was particularly anxious to leave the cabin when the sun rose above the horizon. I gave a lot of thought to our late-night visitor. In spite of our nose-to-nose encounter the previous night, PacMan showed no signs of aggression toward me or Jinda. Maybe the grizzled old bear only looked like a monster. Perhaps he was just another jumbo-sized brownie trying to survive out here like the rest of us.

In spite of his appearance, the calm, confident beast was gracious enough to share his kingdom with the two-legged invaders who had barged their way into his life. In return, we could show the ruler of Redoubt Bay the respect he deserved. We cautiously exited the cabin, looking for any signs of obvious damage. Everything looked intact, except Beatta's eyes widened when she pointed to the ground. The eighteen-inch-long footprint with four-inch claws left in the muddy pathway directly below the porch was proof that PacMan's visit was no illusion.

"That's one big bear," Yeargan exclaimed.

We all nodded our heads in agreement. It was the biggest bear any of us had ever imagined, and we would never forget that night as long as we lived.

Hannah and the Oreos

THE GOLDEN LEAVES of the cottonwood trees outside the lodge signaled the arrival of fall. The cubs were fat and round, and their thick, well-insulated coat that covered their rapidly growing bodies would keep them warm and snug in their winter den. Most of the returning salmon had already spawned, and their decaying corpses littered the bottom of the small inlet at the mouth of Wolverine Creek. Diver, the largest of the three, had also become the breadwinner. Having perfected the art of swimming, he would dive to the bottom of the shallow bay to retrieve the filleted fish carcasses discarded by the fisherman. The young brown bear was now also able to reach the few remaining dead or dying sockeyes lying there gasping their final breaths.

Once the fish was brought to the surface, Diver would swim to the shore. Mama Bear and the other two cubs would be waiting in the shallows, ready to snatch the prize from his jaws. One salmon shared by four hungry bears was quickly devoured. While the anxious trio waited impatiently on the shore, Diver returned to the cold, murky bottom, searching for more fish.

On a few occasions, another large mother bear would also show up at the creek with two-season-old dark-colored cubs. A white blaze across their chest earned them the title of the Oreos.

I dubbed the protective mother Hannah, and she kept the youngsters well away from Diver's family who were usually intent on their next meal, avoiding the newborns. Hannah would scour the creek looking for any tidbits missed by the ravens and gulls. The pickings were slim however, so in the early morning hours, Jinda and I would paddle the canoe across the lake. With Jinda standing guard, I would snag a bucketload of fish with an old treble lure and scatter them along the bank.

PacMan had apparently returned to the open meadows in high country for a final feast of berries and sedges. It would be safer there. The fall hunting season was in full swing, and trophy hunters now replaced the mostly benign fly-fisherman. Whenever a plane touched down on the lake, I would jump in the flat bottom johnboat and hurry across to Wolverine Creek to greet the camo-clad sportsman.

I knew what these guys are, but somehow, shooting a socialized bear from the cockpit of an airplane seemed unethical to me. So I secured a rather-large boom box for these occasions. Opera music blaring from the duo speakers on the would-be wall mounts sent the bears scurrying into the forest. Bears would probably be slaughtered by these self-proclaimed sportsmen, but not my bears. All but one of the trophy-seeking hunters eventually gave up hunting at Redoubt Bay. One man, Rusty Barnes from Soldotna, decided he would pay me a visit at the lodge. He couldn't have picked a worse day.

My good friend and fellow guide, WJ, flew in the previous day to help prepare the cabin and fishing equipment for the upcoming winter season. WJ had dabbled in various forms of self-defense including martial arts, wrestling, and bodybuilding. Although gentle by nature, he also detested trophy hunting and was not one to back away from threats.

I met Rusty at the dock. I knew from previous encounters with this man that he was a loudmouth troublemaker. Jinda, normally friendly to visitors, stood by my side. Staring intently at the gun-touting stranger, her posture was anything but welcoming.

"What can I do for you?" I asked. The tone in my voice reflected the disdain I felt for this cowardly man.

"You're interrupting my hunting season," he bellowed.

"Is that what you call shooting bears from an airplane?" I answered.

The conversation pretty much went tit for tat for the next twenty minutes. Rusty made numerous threats during that time, including burning the cabin down, shooting me, sinking the boats, blah, blah, blah. Unbeknown to me, WJ had been listening to the entire conversation from the generator shed only a few yards away.

"I've got a little wolf bait for your dog there," Rusty added.

Wolf bait, as you may know, is raw meat laced with strychnine and dropped from airplanes. Once consumed, the toxic concoction leads to a slow, excruciating death. Before giving much thought to the consequences of my actions, I lunged forward and grasped the man by the throat. Stronger than he appeared, Rusty was able to knock my hands free. Stumbling backward, he reached down for his sidearm. Just then, Jinda jumped into fray and bit down hard on the man's gunhand. Fearful that my brave dog would be shot, I grabbed her collar and wrenched her backward, attempting to block any possible shot this idiot may be willing to take.

I didn't really even hear him coming, but WJ all but knocked me in the lake when he rushed past. Whatever chance Rusty had of winning this battle just flew out the window. The new contender lifted the man's body completely off the ground and slammed him forcefully into the aircraft. After receiving a crushing blow to the right side of his temple, Rusty's body went limp and crumpled in a heap on the dock. For a moment, I feared he may be dead. But hearing a low moan, the vanquished bully rolled over and tried to lift his swelling head off the ground.

WJ yanked him to his feet, removed his gun belt, then flung the semiconscious fool back into his plane. Looking around briefly for any other weapons, we retrieved the holstered pistol and retreated to the cabin. By the time we got to the house, my entire body was shaking. WJ seemed completely relaxed and went to the kitchen to make a sandwich.

"What should we do now?" I asked him when he returned with his lunch.

"Bury him now or send him on his way," WJ replied, flashing a wicked smile.

For more than an hour, there was no movement at the boat dock, but at last we could hear footsteps coming up the pathway. Before he could knock, I flung the door wide open. Considerably more humble than when he arrived, Rusty politely asked if he could get his gun back. WJ pushed the Eject button on the boom box and, removing the cassette tape, replied, "You can pick it up at the State Trooper's office along with a copy of the tape recording I made while you were blurting out all your threats."

"You know what that means, Mr. Barnes?" he said. "If anything happens to this cabin, the boats, or any of the people living here, the cops will be looking for you."

"And," he continued, "if that dog so much as gets a hangnail, I will personally hunt you down and feed you to the halibut. Any questions?"

Rusty shook his head both up and down and sideways to make certain the man, who tossed him in the air like a rag doll, knew he wouldn't be coming back to make good of his threats.

"I don't ever want to see you on this lake," WJ warned, thereby ending the conversation.

Tossing the tape in my direction, he slammed the door in the man's face. Rusty, looking at the ground, was holding his throbbing head as he walked slowly to the dock, wondering, no doubt, what had gone wrong with his big plan to scare us off. Putting the cassette back in the music box, I looked at my friend quizzically.

"How were you able to tape the whole conversation at the boat dock?" I asked him.

"I didn't," he answered, a big smile spreading across his face. "But he doesn't know that!"

I pushed the Play button, and the sweet sounds of opera music filled the cabin.

The Poacher Sent Packing

THE LONG, COLD winter passed without incident. A red fox made frequent visits to the cabin, looking for voles or digging in the now frozen garden, hoping to unearth any strawberries left on the vines. When weather permitted, Jinda and I would hike up Wolverine Creek to the lake with the same name. Numerous well-worn bear trails made the trek through the Alder and Devil's Club an easy hike. We could make out the trampled beds where the brownies would lie in wait for the salmon's next suicide run.

Wolverine Lake was considerably smaller than Redoubt, but the lack of human visitors here gave it more of a wild, unexplored dimension. The eerie silence was somewhat unsettling, but this was a true, unspoiled wilderness. After making several trips there, it began to feel like home. The wild animals that survive especially under such brutal conditions astound me even today. We followed the tracks of a moose and her two calves browsing in the willows along the lake, having avoided the relentless predators throughout the summer. They would now have to contend with deep snowdrifts and subfreezing temperatures. The odds were unlikely that both calves would survive to adulthood, but these were the harsh laws of nature in its most primal state.

A three-week-long hiatus in Anchorage gave me time to reflect on my decision whether to continue living at the wilderness lodge indefinitely. I wasn't sure if this was indeed an option. My ultimate goals of preserving the few remaining bears at Redoubt seemed unattainable. Laws protecting these animals were vague and unrealistic. This was not an endangered species. A bear in Alaska could be shot and killed for breaking into an ice chest full of beer. Any perceived threat against humans, real or imagined, could end their life. Legally, my hands were tied; and until the laws changed, my interference with the hunting guides could land me in jail.

A state trooper landed his plane on the frozen ice in early spring. I had a pretty good idea why he was there. Rusty Barnes, a local pilot and hunting guide, had put together a committee of "good old boys" to file a complaint against me. My activities at Redoubt Bay were putting a damper on their fun. Although the lawman agreed with my good intentions, he could not condone my methods. My options, he informed me, were limited.

"The threat of going to jail would not help anyone," he assured me.

So I reluctantly agreed to go through all the proper channels rather than take the law into my own hands. Rusty, it turned out, was not exactly on the best of terms with the local fish and wildlife agencies. Numerous charges had been filed on him over the years for everything from poaching to wanton waste of a game animal, but so far, none of the charges filed against him had stuck. For the time being, he was a legal, licensed guide in the state of Alaska; and there was nothing much I could do about it.

I decided to start a letter-writing campaign. There were numerous animal rights organizations here, so perhaps they would be able to help protect the bears at Redoubt Bay. Week after week, I typed away, seeking their advice. A few answered back with appreciation for my plight, but they too were helpless to interfere with state laws protecting wildlife.

Before I knew it, spring came, and then summer returned to Alaska. I began venturing across the lake looking for signs of life. Otis showed up at the cabin one day. His shiny coat suggested he was in good health. In spite of being somewhat underweight, he appeared to have survived the winter quite well.

Jinda recognized her old friend, so rather than run him off, the little dog bowed as if to say she was also happy to see him again. Another black bear also showed up in a meadow adjacent to the property. This one was a female, and by her side were two small cubs. Could these be the offspring of our old friend Otis? I wondered. I could only hope so. The mother bear guarded them carefully and called them with a loud woof when we ventured too closely. I rushed back to the cabin for my camera to document the new arrivals.

On the fourth day of July, salmon predictably returned to their spawning beds, and within hours, three half-grown cubs and the handsome dark-colored sow emerged from the underbrush. Leading the way was no other than Diver. Stepping out on his favorite perch, he surveyed the schooling fish below. A target in sight, the stout young bear launched his body in the air and landed with a giant splash, grappling at the slippery fish with his curved claws. Unsuccessful, he submerged his head in the icy water. When he surfaced, a fat silver coho was locked firmly in his jaws. Wee Bear and Dagger waded in to meet their larger sibling, but this time he remained in the pool and consumed the entire fish without sharing. The freeloading had come to a halt. If the rest of the family intended to eat salmon this summer, they would have to catch them on there own.

Everything went as scheduled. More brown bears arrived at the cramped fishing hole, waiting for the salmon to make a run toward Wolverine Lake. Counting all the cubs, as many as eighteen bears now called Wolverine Creek their home. Occasionally, a fight would erupt among the hungry bruins; but overall, life was peaceful and harmonious. A private plane landed early one morning on the opposite side of the lake.

Awaiting guests, I remained at the dock, minding my own business as promised. A short time later, a shot rang out. Someone was probably warning a bear away from the plane, so I stayed put, hoping for the best. Listening intently, I heard the engine start on the aircraft, and the pilot taxied to the lodge. I waved him over toward the boat dock, and when he exited onto the floats, I could see he was visibly shaken. "We shot a bear," the man stated. "We were trying to scare it away, but my son aimed too low, and I am afraid it was killed." A knot formed in the pit of my stomach. I realized that my worst nightmare had just come true. "Jump in the boat," I said, trying to keep my temper in check. The man and his fifteen-year-old son climbed into the skiff, and firing up the outboard, we dashed to the opposite side of the lake. The boy was wearing a holster, and a large silver pistol was protruding from the scabbard.

"What happened?" I asked.

"When we coasted around the corner of the inlet, we saw this bear walking down the hill by the stream," the young man said. "Dad said to fire over its head to scare it off, but when I shot the gun, the bear kinda jumped sideways and fell in the water."

I could see a large object floating in the general direction the boy was pointing, and using the oars, we paddled toward the lifeless body. When we were closer, I could see the dead animal was just a cub.

"Grab the back leg," I instructed. The boy who had fired the fatal shot moved to the front of the boat, but the father grabbed his shoulder and stopped him.

"I'll do it," he said.

"No!" I insisted. "He pulled the trigger, now he can finish the job." Sensing my building rage, the man didn't argue but sat down, and his careless son reached over the bow and grasped the lifeless animal by the rear leg. I started the outboard, scanned the hillside for a possible enraged sow, and put the motor in reverse. We pulled the dead cub toward a small island a few hundred yards out into the lake, and once safely away from the shoreline, I untied the anchor line and handed it to the man to secure around the small bear's waist. When he pulled the head around, I let out an audible moan.

Mama Bear appeared on the distant shoreline with two cubs by her side. All three bears were staring intently in our direction. The gentle sow, never having threatened a single human being, rose on her hind legs and called for her missing baby. Little Wee Bear, for whatever reason, had taken over the lead to the fishing hole that fateful summer day and had paid the ultimate price.

I covered her body with a tarp and wrestled her still form into the boat. It would take most of the afternoon for the three of us to carry the corpse up to the cabin and dig a grave. I sobbed aloud when she was lowered into the hole, and we began to throw dirt on her body. Without uttering a word, we hauled rocks to the fresh mound of earth to prevent scavengers from digging up the site. When we were finished, I looked at the tear-stained face of the sorrowful young man who had taken the life of this innocent cub.

"I'm so sorry," he said. New tears began to run down his cheeks, and as much as I wanted to comfort him, I couldn't find the words.

"Go home now," I said. "Think about the innocent bear cub that died here today. Next time, leave the gun at home."

"I was afraid we might get attacked," he replied.

"For every bear attack in the United States," I told him, "there are thirty thousand homicides. It's not the bears we need to fear, it's our own kind."

The fisherman and his son left the lake that day with a heavy heart, and I went inside to pack my bags. There was no saving the bears at Redoubt Bay, and it was too painful to stand by and watch them die. I stayed for the summer so not to leave Carl and Kirstin in a bind, but I would begin a new adventure in the spring. It was time to build my own lodge far from my beloved bears, and I would call it Camelot.

Of Wolves and Man

THERE IS NO doubt that any creature on earth has had such a profound impact on humans as the wolf. To the anthropomorphic, the wolf is perceived as a kindred spirit. Indeed, many indigenous cultures consider the wolf as brethren, teacher, and protector. The wolf, some claim, is a spiritual tool put on earth by a higher power to keep nature in balance.

But to a rancher, the wolf might be a manifestation of evil, the hound of the devil, and should be shot on sight. Modern science would suggest that wolves are neither. They are simply wolves, creatures superbly adapted by nature to survive in a manner in which nature intended. But one fact undeniably rings true. Persecution of wolves by humans has eliminated the species by as much as 98 percent in North America and extinct elsewhere. The question now is, can the species that destroyed the wolf find the compassion and exhibit the tolerance to grant this magnificent predator the space it requires and to fulfill its role on earth? It was the wolf in mankind's own beginning that granted our species the knowledge that allowed us to flourish.

*   *   *

For me, the wolf represents not so much as a supreme creation but the true personification of an untethered wilderness. My own well-being, both physically and mentally, is linked to the knowledge that the wilderness exists.

In describing a wolf, are we not in some way also describing our own species? The history of humans and wolves show a parallel universe. Like wolves, our survival requires certain key ingredients. Family is crucial as is a social hierarchy. We are hunters, providers, and guardians. While we bring new life to some, we are a messenger of death to others. Perhaps my own views of nature lean toward the anthropomorphic (putting human emotions in lesser animals), but then I have never perceived the wolf entirely in that way.

*   *   *

Early settlers in North America had an entirely different outlook on the vast wilderness of this new land. They sought not to embrace it but to conquer it. Like the wilderness, the wolf would represent the unknown, and the unknown was feared. The very voice of these wolves, howling mournfully in the dark, would instill a certain terror. Terror could only be silenced in death. A haunting cry of a wolf pack even today conjures up more of the mythological *Canis lupus* than the creature itself. Think for a moment of the fables we read to our children at bedtime. Is it any wonder that the picture we paint in the minds of our young children seldom depicts the wolf itself but more of a reflection of our own troubled realities?

"Heed my words," one author writes. "There lurks in these woods a deceiver of mankind that seeks to devour you."

*   *   *

My own fascination with wolves began at a young age, but this story was not a fable. Some would argue the literary classic *Never Cry Wolf* was not a completely accurate depiction of wolves. Their diet does not consist only of mice. Wolves, like us, are apex predators. But the author Farley Mowat painted a softer picture of wolves in his fascinating novel, but it was that portrayal that would take me to the wilds of Alaska in 1973 in search of phantoms.

*   *   *

The navy recruiter promised me a ticket to the world, so at eighteen years of age, I was ready for the adventure. After completing basic training and eight months of instruction as a hospital corpsman (navy medic), my dream sheet arrived. The first duty station, as I had requested, was Alaska. It was North America's last stronghold of a diverse and powerful predator. The realm of the gray wolf was somewhere in Alaska, but not where I was headed. Adak was a small isolated island far out in the Pacific. I would be closer to wolves in Utah than out here. But for the next twelve months, this would be home although that year I would learn more about the wolves than I ever dreamed.

* * *

Adak was cold, bleak, and dismal. Dating was not an option here although it was well-known that there was a girl hiding behind every tree here. It was also known on Adak that there were no trees, and it was 2,500 miles from nowhere. If I couldn't see a wolf here, I could certainly read everything I could get my hands on about them. The small library on Adak had a plethora of books on everything Alaskan. Back in the early '70s, no topic was more hotly debated than the Alaskan gray wolf.

Caribou/Suki

THE PURPOSE OF writing this book was not to point a finger at any individual or group who may or may not be responsible for the decline of a species. This book, in fact, is not even about saving the planet or the countless species other than mankind that exist here. There are several reputable organizations working diligently worldwide to preserve wildlife and the crucial habitats where endangered species exist. We are all in their debt.

My opinions that I write about are just that, mine. Having spent a considerable amount of time in the deserts, tropical rainforests, and windswept tundras, I base my opinions on my own observations and not on another writer's research. That being said, I return to Alaska and the plight of the Fortymile River caribou herd.

The year was 1974, and construction of the giant oil pipeline from Prudhoe Bay to Fairbank was in full swing. Thousands of workers flocked to the Arctic to make their fortunes on the liquid gold flowing from deep within the frozen tundra. Hunting was a popular pastime for these rugged men. The five hundred thousand population of caribou whose migration route intersected Prudoe Bay's oilfield made it a great sport.

Sadly, in less than a decade, this vast herd would dwindle to less than a few thousand. The indigenous people who relied on caribou for subsistence would go hungry in order to meet the demand for the heads and horns. To this day still, they adorn the walls of every lodge, airport, restaurant, and pool hall from Tok, Alaska, to Dallas, Texas.

Nothing would stand in the way of this petroleum bonanza, and any attempt to stop the massacre of both caribou and wolves in order to appease a small handful of do-gooders would be political suicide. As the caribou numbers drastically declined, drastic steps were taken to locate and destroy the culprits. Anything and everything that preyed on caribou, other than humans, were targeted for extermination; and the number one predator was once more the wolf.

Aerial hunting, trapping, and special government-sponsored programs were used to annihilate wolves in the West. They were implemented not only along the Alaskan pipeline but also throughout Alaska. War was once again waged against the North American gray wolf, but this time the wolf had allies.

Wolf lovers from not only around the country but also around the world raised their voices in protest. But would help arrive in time? Wolf literature lined the shelves of bookstores nationwide. The collective conscience of America was finally awakened. Even hunting organizations that formerly supported selective propagation rallied for the wolf. Suddenly, a new strategy came into play. The buzzword changed from culling to biodiversity. Wildlife, it was decided, belonged to all Americans. Not just to a select few.

Although the history lessons regarding errors in wildlife management, such as the disappearance of Bison on the plains of North America a century ago, were slow in coming. Progress was being made in the early eighties, and the wolf had at last come full circle. Most Americans and the world as a whole no longer perceived wolves as another disposable species. The wolf was once more a kindred spirit.

The working title for the movie was called *Shadow Chasers*. It was a far-fetched story of a small boy who was being raised in the wilderness by a pack of wolves. Unlike the movies in the past, this production company wished to remain politically correct by portraying the wolf as the hero and not the villain. The year was 1986, and wolves were at the top of the popularity ratings. Everywhere you looked, it was wolf. Wolf T-shirts, wolf posters, wolf tapestries, and of course, wolf movies. They were looking for a stuntman approximately the same height and weight as the lead actor in the film.

They also needed someone foolish enough to let a grown wolf weighing approximately one hundred and sixty pounds tackle him in a rocky meadow while holding a large hunk of raw, bloody meat in his hand. Looking back, I don't remember negotiating a price for the stunt or even inquiring as to whether my medical expenses would be covered should my hand be inadvertently loped off. I just said yes.

I'd been working in the movie industry as an exotic-animal trainer since the late seventies but was hired for this gig by a company located in the Mojave Desert about an hour east of Los Angeles. This family-run business had been in operation for many years; and to this day, I have never met a kinder, more ethical group of animal lovers in my life. Everyone living on the facility, both humans and animals alike, were treated like family. Little did I know at the time that they would be some of the most influential people in my life.

At any given time, you might find a bear tethered in the font yard, a lynx resting on the front porch, or a screech owl named Wookie glaring down from his perch on the overhead light. One day the tigers would be wrestling in the spacious compound, and the next day it might be wolves or mountain lions.

Poncho, the jaguar, or his playmate Serena, the lioness, had a large pool to swim in. Eva, the olive baboon, lounged on the couch in the office. This was Cougar Hill Ranch, and its reputation for training wild animals for the movie industry was known far and wide. Wolves were their specialty, and no one knew wolves better than Nick, Helena, and Elizabeth Toth. Nick and Elizabeth were brother and sister and had been raised working with animals. Helena was their aunt, and a finer exotic-animal trainer would never be found.

The founder, George Toth, emigrated from Hungary in the early seventies and was legendary in his remarkable ability to interact with almost any species from birds of prey to the biggest of bears. George's tragic death in 1985 left an empty void in the lives of all that knew him. Cougar Hill Ranch's large pack of trained wolves was in constant demand, and one of the very best was Suki.

Suki was a no-nonsense kind of wolf, and he had little tolerance for a would-be rookie stuntman who couldn't get the shot right on the first take. We rehearsed the stunt a few times in the compound at the ranch prior to doing it on film.

"Hold the stick with the meat attached to the end," Helena would say. "When Suki runs towards you, press the buzzer in your hand to get his attention. When he is about ten feet away, raise your hands over your head like you're blocking the attack. Then fall down on the ground like you've been tackled by a linebacker. Any questions?"

"Hell yeah, I've got questions," I fired back. The reality of what I had just signed for was finally sinking into my thick skull. "Does Suki understand the ground rules here?" I asked.

I walked the amazing wolf in the open desert surrounding the ranch on numerous occasions, but I'd never had him on top of me. He was everything you would expect from an Arctic wolf: tall, elegant, and graceful. The long gray guard hairs covering his muscular frame would rise and fall like the mane on a wild mustang with every flowing step he took.

Elizabeth would remind me, "Suki is trained. He's not tame. Wolves will always be inherently wild animals. So always watch your back."

Suki had accepted me well enough, but I wasn't about to push my luck especially with twenty-five hundred pounds of jaw pressure and long, powerful canine teeth that were capable of hamstringing a grown elk. This was one animal you didn't want around you if he was having a bad day. While attaching a chain around the wolf's powerful neck, he would sometimes emit a deep rumbling growl from deep within his chest. It was a subtle reminder from Suki as to who was walking who.

The sweet fragrance of ponderosa pine hung in the air when we arrived on the set. The assistant director (AD), Pamela, met us in the parking lot and immediately began firing off questions the moment we stepped from the truck.

"How was the drive? You brought the wolf, right? Is this our stuntman?"

The sun was barely peeking over the Sierra foothills, and already this woman was wound up tighter than a rattlesnake in December. We had been driving most of the night from Southern California almost to the Oregon border, and this woman was quickly becoming a nuisance.

"We'll need to get you to wardrobe," she exclaimed, looking me up and down. Nick stepped from the truck yawning. He was accustomed to dealing with impatient movie crews. Ignoring Pamela, he looked at his sister.

"Liz," he said, "you and Terry get Suki out of the trailer to stretch his legs, but don't go too far.

Pamela, looking down at her clipboard, chimed in, "I'm not ready for the wolf yet."

Nick, with the slightest bit of irritation in his voice, interrupted, "That's good." He said, "He's probably not ready for you either. Where can we find a cup of coffee and something to eat?"

"Oh, follow me. I'm sure they're still serving breakfast. We should discuss the first shot while you eat."

Nick glanced at the clipboard in mock interest. "Lead the way," he said.

Suki was fed a light meal and given a bucket of fresh water. He seemed more interested in exploring the forest and marking every tree in sight than eating. So with Suki in the lead, off we went.

Wolves, like most members of the canid family, explore the world not so much with their eyes as they do with their nose. While humans have around 5,000 scent receptors in their nostrils, a wolf has more than 350,000. Suki, by merely sniffing the ground outside the trailer, processed the individual smell of everyone and everything that had passed by that location in the past ten days.

Moving silently across the thick layer of pine needles that carpeted the forest floor, Suki would stop frequently to take in all of the new and unusual smells. Every bird and every beast leaves behind their own faint telltale fingerprint. And Suki could detect them all. This was once wolf country although wolves had been eradicated from this region of northern California more than a century ago. The ghosts of these forgotten legends still lingered in the air, and Suki rejoiced in their haunted past by rolling lavishly in a blanket of fallen leaves.

When we returned to the set, Nick greeted us with a freshly made breakfast burrito and a carton of orange juice.

"We only have a few minutes," he said. "You'll have to 'wolf it' down." Always the jokester, Nick could always incite a laugh. Even at this early hour.

"Where's Liz?" he asked.

Liz, or Elizabeth as she was formerly known, seldom spoke above a whisper. She had an uncanny ability to read an animal's thoughts and emotional state of mind with the soft touch of her hand.

"I think she and Suki are snuggling in the warm hay in the back of the trailer." Suki adored Liz and would listen intently to her every word.

"I'll go get her."

"No!" Nick said. "You need to get to wardrobe. You're up in about twenty minutes."

Liz entered the clearing from the direction of the honey wagon, which is Hollywood's version of a portable toilet.

"I thought you went back to bed with Suki," I said.

"I considered it," she answered. "But he snores worse than you do."

The assistant director approached in her usual flurry.

"Where is our stuntman?" she asked. I reluctantly raised my hand and walked in her direction. At this point, I could more accurately be described as a human sacrifice. Typical of every movie set I have ever worked on, the order of the day was hurry and wait. I stuffed the last bite of burrito in my mouth and headed in the direction of organized chaos.

Call time for animal trainers was usually the crack of dawn. That means you had to be packed and ready to go by five, on the road by six, and on the set for the sunrise shot by seven in the morning. What usually transpired, however, was being put on standby till eleven thirty and then pressured to get the shot by noon so everyone could break for lunch, leaving the trainers wondering why we ever got up before the rooster crowed, just to stand around waiting as usual.

Location shoots like this one was typically more relaxed. Watching Suki explore the forest that morning was well worth the long all-night drive. I still remember him running in circles.

Whether she didn't hear me or simply chose to ignore the comment, Pamela spun military-style in an about-face and, taping her shiny new clipboard, announced to the world, "We have to get you over to wardrobe."

Assuming it was me she was referring to, I fell in line behind the now rapidly departing AD to once more witness the everyday hustle and bustle of another Hollywood production. A series of trailers formed a semicircle in the small clearing at the edge of the trees. One of them had a long clothing rack near the front door.

So this was the famous wardrobe I had been hearing so much about. It reminded me of my sister Jody's last garage sale in Fairbanks.

Most of the apparel was hung according to size, and there were two racks that appeared to be gender specific. We waited momentarily while the young lady in charge of outfitting the cast of the movie nodded in our direction. She had a pleasant smile and, unlike everyone else around her, didn't appear to be rushed.

"What do we have here, Pamela?" she asked.

"This is our double for Mr. Dugan." Pamela was attempting to introduce me but realized she hadn't ever asked me my name.

"I'm Terry." I extended my hand. "Terry Moore. It's very nice to meet you."

"Cheryl," she said. She held my hand firmly while making her assessment of my approximate wardrobe requirements. "Five foot nine inches," she guessed. "And about one hundred and seventy-five pounds."

If I didn't know better, I'd think she did this for a living. I liked this woman. She was probably a local. Way too friendly for a Southern California chick.

Pamela suddenly chimed in, "You should see the beautiful wolf they brought. He has the biggest feet."

"Paws," Cheryl corrected, "wolves have paws." Pamela seemed unimpressed with the woman's knowledge of wolf anatomy and departed with her final instructions.

"On the set in ten minutes," she ordered. "I'll be back in eight."

Cheryl thumbed through the rack of men's clothing and removed an outfit that looked to be about my size.

"Try these on," she said.

"Where do I change?"

"In your trailer, of course."

She pointed in the direction of two trailers that were adjacent to the wardrobe trailer.

"Yours is the one on the right."

There are dog people in the world, and then there are those who fancy cats. Cheryl was the former, I wagered, probably favored Labradors. I pictured her snuggled by a campfire with a large retriever lying at her feet. Pamela most likely had a goldfish or possibly a caged bird. Those were the type of pets that required the least amount of attention. Lord knows she had little time in her life for a meaningful relationship. She was too busy handing out orders.

I walked over to the two trailers. The one on the right was considerably larger and had a custom-made placard framed in oak with two gold stars on either side of the stenciled name: *DENNIS DUGAN.*

This must be the actor I would be doubling, I thought. I was certainly no expert on celebrities, but I certainly never heard of a Dennis Dugan. It turned out that Mr. Dugan was a little-known actor who had appeared in a few B-rated movies. And staying true to form, he was now starring in another one. But at least on this one, he had his own trailer. I wanted to take a peek inside but resisted the temptation. Besides, I had my own dressing room. But judging by its diminished size and the hand-written sign on the door, it probably wasn't nearly as lavish as the no-name actor's.

At least, I thought, they spelled my name right. No gold stars, no middle initial. I walked inside and opened the small window over the double bed. In the hallway stood a full-length mirror, and a small table in the kitchen area contained two mismatched folding chairs. Although the linoleum floor had peeled around the edges, I still felt somewhat spoiled. This may be a no-name production company starring a no-name actor, but at least I wasn't changing my clothes out in the forest.

I wished for a moment that my older half brother, Patrick, could see me now. While growing up, I seldom see my older sibling. He was nearly grown by the time I made my first appearance on earth. I can recall a few brief visits, but I assumed all family members were as distant and uncaring as were my own. Even when I was sent to live in a foster home after the death of my mother when I was seven years of age, it never dawned on me that my brother might take me in. He did visit once however.

I was living on a boys' ranch in the one-horse town of Birdseye, Utah. It was the seventh foster home I had been transferred to, and this was by far my favorite. I was now sixteen years old, and I remember the brief visit vividly. One of the other boys, Kenneth, caught up with me in a pasture by a flowing creek.

"You have a visitor," he said. "I think it's your brother."

"Not me," I replied. "I don't have a brother. Are you sure he's here to see me?"

"I think his name is Pat."

I was dumbfounded. I wouldn't even know what to say to the man, but I followed Kenneth back to the house anyway. Patrick looked considerably smaller than I remembered and had almost no hair left on the top of his crown. We shook hands briefly, and he introduced me to his latest girlfriend.

"How's Connie and the kids?" I asked.

He scowled and chose to ignore the inquiry I had made about his wife of eleven years and their two young boys. The woman appeared embarrassed and looked at the ground. I remember she was quite attractive, and I wondered what she would see in a man who let strangers raise and care his own brother while his own house sat empty. His two sons were being raised by his now ex-wife in a small apartment in East Salt Lake. Patrick was free as a bird and had apparently come here to strut. We visited for perhaps fifteen minutes, and then my long-lost brother made a hasty retreat. He would never return.

As I looked around the small trailer with the full-length mirror and double bed, I wondered why I would've cared if my brother approved or disapproved of my chosen vocation.

Perhaps it was just to say, "I'm still here, Patrick. I made it without you."

I stretched out on the bed after carefully removing my boots.

Hey, I thought, I could get used to this star treatment. Well, maybe it wasn't exactly star treatment, but at least they spelled my name correctly. I rose to my feet and changed into my new wardrobe. The shirt was a little tight, but I wouldn't be wearing it long enough to worry about it. A knock on the door alerted me to the fact that my life of luxury was over. Pamela, as promised, had returned; and with clipboard still in hand, she was on a mission.

"Ready?" she asked. Spinning on her heels, she didn't wait for my reply.

I took one final look in the mirror and followed the AD toward the set. The clothing that I had arrived in was folded neatly on the bed. Old habits die hard. I smiled.

Pamela's next comment would stop me in my tracks. "We have to get you to makeup."

"Hold on a minute there, lady," I argued. "Don't get me wrong now. I like makeup. I like it on girls. I like it on the little old ladies in church. Hell, I even like makeup on clowns. But ain't nobody putting makeup on this cowboy."

"A little homophobic, are we?" she chided.

"No, it's not that I'm overly macho. I may not be as in touch with my feminine side as I should be. But makeup is out."

Eyeliner on men may be fashionable in Hollywood, but this wasn't LA. My brief stand-in for Mr. Dugan would not require any application on my person of products manufactured by Maybelline, Estée Lauder, or Cover Girl.

"I have a reputation to uphold," I insisted. I'm not sure what my reputation was at that point, but I wasn't about to tarnish it with lipstick and blush.

"This is silly," she said. "Your hair is entirely too dark. And the hair color washes right out."

I didn't know what all the fuss was about since for most of the shot, I'd be wearing a wolf on my head, but I guess a little hair coloring wouldn't hurt. Now the hard part. Nick would have a ball once he got a look at my outfit. And I'd never live down the blond hair, but that was Hollywood. To my surprise, it wasn't Nick who let loose on me. It was Nellie.

"Well, don't you look pretty?"

"Don't you start on me," I warned. "I know where you keep your expired green card, and I heard they're paying a bounty for illegal immigrants."

Nellie, born under the name of Helena Walsh, was a product of Ireland. She moved to the United States over twenty years earlier, and in spite of my taunting, Helena was as American as I was and I loved her like a sister. During my many years at Cougar Hill Ranch, she would prove herself to be my dearest friend.

Attack of the Great White Wolf

AS EXPECTED, SHORTLY before the noon hour, we were called to the set. The director approached us cautiously and for a good reason, Suki was leading the way.

"Is he friendly?" he asked.

The director stopped a few yards short of actual contact. Nick was always hesitant to let the public get too close to the animals but answered the question in a diplomatic fashion.

"Suki loves people." But before the man could step forward, he added, "Wolves greet you with their mouth, so you have to be careful. They don't realize how thin-skinned we are."

Nick was right. Wolves greet each other by grasping each other's muzzle in their mouth. Some of this behavior is a form of dominance, but it may also be that they have such a damn hard time shaking hands. Either way, it's always best to keep civilians at bay when working with wild animals on a set. Once the first person comes up, before you know it, you're surrounded by the entire cast and crew, all wanting to pet the wolf. There's always one person who insists on crawling around on the ground in what they presume is the correct way to greet wild animals. This unorthodox behavior is usually accompanied by whines and whimpers and even an occasional howl. And that even doesn't include the sounds the wolf makes.

I remember an education program I was conducting for a group of seniors in Anchorage, Alaska, in the summer of '88. I was working with a beautiful dark black wolf named Sidra. The wolves and humans exhibit was in town for three months. I had been hired to manage the exhibit and help interpret the various displays. This was a world-class interactive display designed and built by the Science Museum of Minnesota. The various booths in the ten-thousand-foot exhibit would take the visitor on a tour that depicted human-wolf interaction from the dawn of time.

On this particular day, a large group of senior citizens touring Alaska had requested a private tour of the exhibit. The leader of the group was a gentleman by the name of James Fox. Besides the tour, he also inquired as to where we might obtain a live wolf to show the group since all the wolves in the displays were as he described them "mannequins with manes."

Jim hailed from Tampa, Florida, and claimed to be somewhat of a resident expert on the red wolf (*Canis rufus*). Red wolves are a smaller cousin to the gray wolf that once roamed the southern portion of the United States. They are now confined to a few isolated pockets and have possibly inbred with coyotes and domestic dogs. Some experts feel they were no longer even a viable species. After touring the various displays, the group was escorted to a large meeting room in an adjacent building. A stage had been erected for a previous group, so once the group was comfortably seated, I stepped up to the podium to briefly address them and answer any questions. Most of the questions revolved around the Alaskan gray wolf controversy, which was an extremely hot topic at that time.

While answering a question regarding my opinion on aerial hunting of wolves, Jim, who was seated in the front row, suddenly bound to his feet and, with a clap of his hands, announced to the group that "we" would now be bringing a wolf in. The "we" he was referring to, I assumed, meant he and I.

I can only guess that having been born with the name Fox (another canid species), he somehow felt he had inherited a natural ability to interact with all members of that genus in such a manner they would instinctually consider him part of the pack.

Jim instructed the group to remain in their seats and no one with the exception of him or me were to approach the wolf. He rambled on about the inherent danger he would be facing on their behalf but that it was his great honor to assist in this valuable education. Not wishing to embarrass my canine-loving colleague, I asked if he could help me assemble the leash and other equipment located in the back. He assured me he had my back, and with that, we stepped out the door. The moment the door closed, I informed Mr. Fox for insurance purposes that guests were not allowed to handle the animals. Still not realizing that I was referring to him, he assured me no one in the group would consider defying his authority and I need not worry. This was going all wrong, so I tried a different approach.

"Jim," I said, "as you know, wolves can be a little testy with strangers. If I can count on you to back me up, we will go ahead and get Sidra out of the truck." This was my polite way of saying stay out of the way.

"I'm ready," he replied. "I'll get the door."

"Hey." I thought he was finally catching on.

Expecting him to return to the door, which we had just come through, he instead walked to the truck housing Sidra. Grasping the door handle, Jim then attempted to yank it open. He assumed, I suppose, that Sidra would just magically follow him back into the room and lay comfortably at his feet.

Too close for comfort, I thought, so I informed Jim I would not require his assistance. For a moment, he stared at me in disbelief and retreated indignantly back to the room, slamming the stage door in his wake.

Better safe than sorry, I said to myself.

I hoped I had not embarrassed him, but Sidra was a large and powerful animal, and I had assured her owner that I wouldn't allow anyone to get hurt. For the next forty uncomfortable minutes, I entertained the small group of senior citizens from Florida. Everyone seemed to thoroughly enjoy the program, everyone with the exception of Mr. Fox. He had relocated to the very back of the room. His interest in wolves, it seemed, had faded.

Sidra went on to entertain and enlighten countless audiences for years to come. Wolf lovers from seven years old to seventy all gained a new appreciation for this amazing animal. She was, without a doubt, a true ambassador for her species.

*   *   *

You are probably wondering if we are going to get around to finishing the story I began. So forgive my ramblings and return with me back to *Shadow Chasers* and the great white wolf.

A small wooden disc called a mark was placed on the ground between two towering pines. This was the spot Suki would make his first appearance. I was placed approximately seventy-five feet away in an open meadow. In my hand was a small pencil-sized stick with a buzzer attached to the end. On the opposite end of the stick hung a bloody piece of raw meat the size of a Ping-Pong ball. The idea was simple. Call Suki with the buzzer, and when he was close, raise it above my head to encourage him to jump for the bait.

"Roll camera," came the announcement.

While I was still mulling everything over in my mind everything that could go wrong, I failed to notice the scene was moving forward without me. Like a phantom, Suki emerged from the trees. Being the brilliant animal actor he was, he went directly to the partially covered disc. With flicking of the fingers on her right hand and with a quiet voice command, Nellie gave the signal for the trained snarl. "Suki, big smile."

The wolf lifted his lips, exposing the massive canines. They were visible even from that distance.

"Action," the director whispered, pointing to me. In a nervous response to the flashing fangs, I inadvertently squeezed my fist thereby ringing the dinner bell. Suki sprang into action, but before I could react, the wolf raced across the open field and was standing before me looking for the bait.

Raise your hands, I said to myself; but before I could lift my arms above me, Suki spotted the bait and, jumping up, planted both saucer-sized paws squarely on my chest. In what appeared like a schoolyard bully stealing lunch money from his classmate, he pushed me onto my rump. The so-called wolf attack was well embarrassing.

"Cut," yelled the director, glaring at me in frustration.

"Sorry," I said, thoroughly embarrassed by the entire event.

Liz stepped in throwing a pickup rope around Suki as I looked at Helena for salvation.

"Can we try that again?" I whispered as I stood upright to my entire diminished height of ten inches just when someone in the back yelled,

"Hell, my dog can do a better attack than that."

Nick faced the heckler and hurled a challenge.

"Bring along the wife and kids, and you will have a whole pack."

"Quiet on set." The director was beginning to get annoyed and for a very good reason. Pamela stepped in and whispered to the director a suggestion that proved to be a great idea.

"If I saw a wolf standing in the trees snarling at me, I wouldn't wait to be attacked. I'd run like hell."

"Try running this time," he said as Suki was placed back on the mark and the camera repositioned.

"Action." This time I was ready.

Dog this, I thought, looking briefly into the group of bystanders. As Suki rushed forward, I glanced back over my shoulder. Twenty feet to go, but about the time I reached full stride, Suki launched into a fifteen-foot leap at the bait positioned over my head. This time, the airborne wolf initiated a full-on tackle that would have made a Dallas Cowboys linebacker envious. I can't be sure how far forward I was propelled, but if you've ever been hit by a fat man riding his kids' snowboard while trying to outrun an avalanche, you'll probably be coming close.

Looking up at the director's face while spitting dirt and pine needles from my mouth, I was certain we got the shot.

"Cut. Print. Nice work. Let's break for lunch."

Suki was returned to the trailer and fed the remainder of his breakfast. After eating, he was watered and brushed down. We headed over to craft services' lunch wagon. A voice behind me sounded worried.

"You all right?" Nellie asked, brushing five pounds of forest floor from my wardrobe.

"Sure, I feel great," I responded. "I'm just glad the rest of you finally got your acts together."

We all had a good laugh over the first attempt at a wolf attack that failed. There were a few pats on the back from the crew at lunch, and even the man with the *now-famous flying dog* came up with a feeble congrats.

"Nice hit. You looked like you were really trying to get away."

"Looking at Suki standing in the trees with saliva running from his snarling jowls," I said, "I wasn't exactly looking forward to the tackle."

The banter, I suppose, was his attempt at an unspoken apology. But the following morning, feeling bruised and battered, I wished we could have rehearsed the scene with a slightly smaller wolf. I returned to the trailer to change back into my own clothes. My name had been erased from the board, but the box of chalk was left on the stairs. Picking out the largest piece, I carefully drew two white stars on either side of the only great actor to appear on this flick, Suki, the wolf. No last name, no middle initial.

Life on the Fortymile River

IN THE MID-1980S, a writers strike had all but crippled Hollywood. The few movies and commercials being produced were often low-budget films and often did not involve the cost-prohibitive luxury of exotic animals. I had stayed in contact with my older sister, Jody. She had run off to Alaska when she was sixteen years old. Barefoot and pregnant, Jody was about to embark on a journey that would bring her not only the greatest joy she had ever known but also the biggest heartache.

John Burns was her high school sweetheart and father of her baby and would soon become her husband. When they met, sparks flew, and before long the two were inseparable. They became so inseparable that when Jody entered her senior year, a noticeable change began to take place in my gregarious sibling. John's father was living in Wasilla, a small town outside of Anchorage. While residing in the nether reaches of Alaska, the two high schoolers continued their in-depth studies of the human anatomy and reproductive process of the human body. An early pregnancy was probably not the desired outcome they had hoped for.

She invited me to come to Anchorage for a visit, so in late May, I headed north. It would prove to be an unforgettable adventure. Summers in Alaska are as spectacular as anywhere in the world. But summers in Anchorage, Alaska's largest city, are like summers in any busy city. The brief summer season results in a huge influx of tourists. Visitors from far and wide flood the cities, rivers, hotels, and airports. Fishermen and a host of other outdoor enthusiasts would flock to the Last Frontier for a chance to experience North America's raw, untamed wilderness.

Instead, they found the same traffic jams, crowds, and chaos they left behind when they started the journey. The world-class fishing on the famous Kenai River was a mass of flailing rods with fishermen standing elbow to elbow. Four to five deep, they hurled insults to their fellow anglers as traffic went bumper-to-bumper. You get the picture.

If you can drive to it, so can the two million other people who left before you did. Any wildlife, say a bear and her cubs scouring the riverbank for a fisherman's lost salmon, quickly scampers off into the forest at the arrival of the first human intrusion. But the true Alaska was still there as vast and as majestic as your wildest dreams. To get there, you need to fly; so if you are a local, you know where to go to get to that secret, guarded fishing hole on some unnamed river with a sandbar.

Some runways in the Alaska bush are just long enough to land a small two-man bush plane to land on. A comical bumper sticker commonly seen in the frozen north reads, "My other car is a Cessna." If the lower forty-eight is where you call home, then Rust's flying service was one of many other small taxi-by-air companies that spring up at the beginning of every summer. Rust's pilots fly visitors into Alaska's vast interior where the only endangered species might be you. They also have a bumper sticker: "There Are Old Pilots and There are Bold Pilots: But there are no Old, Bold Pilots!" But Alaska's bush pilots are the finest aviators anywhere in the world. I would learn this firsthand in the not-so-distant future, but for now, I was city bound. I would enjoy my time reliving the old days as well as the troubled childhood we left behind.

After a couple of weeks visiting Jody, it was time to escape the confines of Anchorage and head into the bush. Now the bush, for any of you wannabe sourdoughs, is anywhere in Alaska that is only accessible by floatplane, dog team, or one hell of a long walk. Having neither the time nor the financial resources to fly into the wilderness, I opted for door number 3.

My sister's closest and dearest friends had a small cabin located on a small tributary of the Yukon River. The Fortymile River was not named for the actual length of the river itself but for the number of back-breaking miles of bumpy dirt roads you had to drive to get there. During the great gold rush of 1856, a handful of prospectors who were panning for gold hit the mother lode. The tidal wave of gold seekers who followed often carried no more than a pick or a shovel. Those with better sense brought along a gold pan and a rifle.

For the most part, the hopeful prospectors, with little more than the clothes on their back, trekked the long and difficult journey to the banks of the Fortymile River, seeking their fortune. Soon an entire town was constructed in the once-virgin forest, complete with a hotel, a saloon, even a crudely built bank, and a jail. Chicken, Alaska, as the settlement became known, is still tucked away in the forest. Ghosts haunt the decaying structures of this once-booming gold town where fortunes were made and lost and legendary pioneers risked life and limb to scratch out an existence in this hostile environment.

Jim Brown was a modern-day prospector, but pick and shovel had been replaced with a Keene Dredge and a dry suit. Any gold that remained in the Fortymile was beneath the massive boulders or deep in granite cracks and crevasses far beyond the reach of the rudimentary tools of the original prospectors of days gone by. Donning the wet suit, he dove to the bottom of the icy cold river. Jim would drag a long hose that was attached to a twenty-five-horsepower motor. The cumbersome device basically operated like a giant shop vac. Anything smaller than eighth inch in diameter of the hose (sand, gravel, leaves, and even the occasional Arctic grayling) was sucked up the long hose and ran across a sluice box that collected the gold. Everything went back in the river.

Of course, the Arctic grayling were saved for the frying pan. Grayling are not only a great fish to catch on an ultralight fly rod, but they are also one of the finest eating fish you can find. The gravel, which was returned to the river, was completely gold free and would be redistributed with the next big rainstorm. By the end of summer, the Fortymile River returned to its original form.

Even with the wet suit, the frigid glacial-fed river was too cold to endure for more than an hour or two. So the remaining twenty-two hours of daylight was spent sleeping, eating, or playing another hand of cribbage. In the land of the midnight sun, there was also ample time to explore the old ghost town. A once-thriving community, it now only had dilapidated structures that serve as comfortable dens for hibernating black bears or an occasional porcupine.

There was other wildlife here as well. Willow ptarmigan, small grouse somewhat smaller than a chicken, are plentiful in and around the Fortymile. The town, Chicken, was named after this tasty fowl. But early prospectors couldn't spell ptarmigan, pronounced tar-ma-gin, so they referred to the bird and the town as the next closest thing – chickens. At that time, Chicken, Alaska, had a summer population of around seventy-five residents and a winter population of four, counting Molly and Jake, the two golden retrievers that kept Chicken's only year-round human residents company throughout the long winter and short summer.

Moose fox, brown bears, and wolverines patrolled the surrounding forests and bogs. On occasion, the haunting cry of a resident wolf pack would make its rounds and could be heard in the surrounding wilderness. Secretive by nature, these wolves were seldom seen. But on one rare occasion, I would encounter these remarkable predators. It was an experience I would never forget.

Jim was fixing the floats on the dredge that morning, so I ventured deep into the forest. The previous night, we listened to the wolves howling not far from the cabin. Taking the boat to the opposite side of the shallow river, I secured the small craft to a sapling and crept silently through the trees. Armed with only a can of pepper spray, I worked my way deeper and deeper into the forest in the general direction of the last diminishing calls heard the previous night. There were grizzlies here, and thinking it foolish to be creeping around in the woods where a chance encounter might lead to an unprovoked attack, I removed the canister of pepper spray from its holster. A feeble deterrent at best, pepper spray had effectively repelled bears elsewhere in the lower forty-eight, but those were black bears. A slap on the rump could send black bears on their way, but grizzlies were an entirely different critter.

I refused to carry a firearm, so pepper spray would have to suffice. It was eerily silent as I hiked deeper into the trees. The mossy forest floor muffled my footsteps. The drone of an aircraft engine could be heard far off in the distance, but soon it too faded. A large black bird flapped its wings overhead and spiraled downward, disappearing into a clearing a couple hundred yards ahead. Ravens were common throughout Alaska. These omnivorous birds were often seen scavenging the remains of mammals killed by the larger carnivores. Moving cautiously through the trees, I approached an opening in the canopy and watched for any movements.

Several ravens were perched on the far side of the clearing, staring intently at the ground below. What remained of a moose carcass was lying in the tall grass halfway across the open meadow. Only two carnivores were capable of bringing down an adult moose, and one of them would probably be guarding the kill. Gripping the canister tightly in my hand, I knelt down in the shadows of the stunted pine trees. The ravens were hesitant to leave their perch, which meant only one thing. Whatever killed the moose was still close by. Until I was certain of its location, I wasn't getting any closer. Wolves posed no threat to me. In fact, no human had ever been attacked by a wild wolf either here in Alaska or anywhere in North America. I did, however, not wish to run the wolves off their kill. A prey this large was dangerous to bring down even for a pack of wolves. There would likely be pups to feed this time of year, so I settled down in the trees, waiting to see what would appear.

Alaska versus Wolf

THERE WERE SEVEN wolves in all. The large alpha male appeared first. I guessed his height at around three feet tall at the shoulder. His entire coat was silvery gray and may have weighed more than one hundred pounds. Lifting his rear leg, he marked a towering spruce tree, thereby identifying this as his territory. A wolf packs' home range might encompass fifty square miles or more, and a pack would consistently travel throughout it on a constant search for their next meal. Three more wolves emerged silently from the forest. One appeared to be limping, possibly sustaining an injury while bringing down the nearby moose. It's a dangerous game tackling such large prey, but a game the old male wolf had played many times before. The last three remaining wolves from this sizable pack entered into the clearing.

A large female approached the moose carcass cautiously. With my binoculars, I could make out the swollen teats indicating a den was nearby. Wolves seldom ventured far from newborn pups. She also marked, signifying she was the alpha male's mate and second in command. All of the wolves, with the exception of the alpha female, had distended stomachs indicating they had gorged on the kill. The female had most likely regurgitated her meal to feed the growing pups. They would remain in the safety of the burrow while the pack went in search of the next meal. Each kill would sustain not only the pack but also the growing pups. At last she began to feed, gulping down large chunks of meat. The still-satiated pack lounged nearby in the shade.

They were probably from a previous litter or just part of the pack that had survived the long, harsh winter. Wolf pelts were selling for a record four hundred dollars each that year, so in addition to all the natural pitfalls that might befall an inexperienced, youthful wolf, mankind was still its greatest threat. One of the almost completely black wolves rose to his feet and timidly approached the kill, tucking his tail tight to his rump. Laying his ears back as a sign of submission, he stepped tentatively toward the feast before him. The hackles on the large female wolves bristled, and a low growl rumbled from her chest. The subordinate slunk to the ground. There would be no feeding on the remains of the moose kill until the alpha female had her fill. No one, save the old male, would challenge her authority.

I dared not move from my secluded blind. Even a flinch would be detected. But I had already remained motionless for more than an hour, and the feeling in my legs was beginning to fade. Unexpectedly, the wind shifted, and the faint breeze that had thus far been in my favor now carried my scent toward the pack. The large male suddenly became alert.

If there was any chance of getting a picture of the pack, it was now or never. I brought the camera to my face and zoomed in on the pack leader. Then adjusting the focus, I snapped a single photo before the entire family melted back into the forest. I remained frozen in place for what seemed like an hour in the hopes of the pack returning; but they would have no way of knowing, unlike the rest of my kind, I meant them no harm. When I returned to the clearing two days later, little was left of the carcass. Only some of the moose hide and some larger bones were found. These few scraps would be eventually consumed by the smaller scavengers.

I returned to camp late in the evening to share my incredible adventure with Jim. Jim Brown was a true Alaskan outdoorsman who knew the wilderness and all of its inhabitants intimately. Although we were friends, our love of the outdoors varied greatly. During the winter months, he ran a trapline on the Fortymile River just north of Fairbanks. Wildlife was a commodity to Jim, and many others shared his way of thinking. Their mind-set was that the wolf was something to be harvested like a crop and sold to the highest bidder.

Currently, Europe was the fur capital of the world, and wolf pelts were prized above all others. I could only pray my new wolf friends, who allowed me into their world for just a short-lived moment, would remain safely hidden from the dangers that threatened their survival. Perhaps, the day will come when creatures, like the Alaskan gray wolf, will be granted the right to exist on their own terms as they had existed for thousands of years before mankind's dominion over all living things interrupted the natural cycle.

I returned to Anchorage at summer's end. The hustle and bustle of the busy city felt foreign and unnatural; but it was the world I had been born into, and in many ways, it also felt like home. I was, like it or not, a modern man; and unlike the wolf, civilization was where I felt I belonged. I was anxious to develop the pictures I had taken if for no other reason than to relive the fleeting glimpse into the world of balanced species that existed and belonged there.

Whenever I thumb through my photo album, the photo of the silver wolf makes me yearn for one last adventure into the Alaskan wilderness and the magic that exists there even now.

The Island Wolves

IN 1985, THERE was one last Alaskan wolf adventure that not only introduced me to a rare and unique subspecies of *Canis lupus* but also gave me the privilege of meeting one of the most knowledgeable and fascinating wolf biologists on the western hemisphere. Bob Ballard incurred a fascination with wolves in his sophomore year of college. The University of Minnesota was at the forefront of the wolf debate. It is in fact the only other state in the union with a viable population of wolves besides Alaska. Following in the footsteps of a man who was arguably the leading authority on wolves in North America, David Meech wrote the book on the gray wolves of Minnesota and had been both a mentor and an inspiration to Bob.

For two previous summers, the chain of islands located in Southeast Alaska was where Bob conducted valuable research on the archipelago wolves. Ironically, he had been hired by the Alaska Department of Fish and Game, which historically had been more instrumental in killing wolves than preserving them. But if his research was successful, Bob's work would help to determine if these smaller cousins of the wolves on the mainland were descendants of the red wolf (*Canis rufus*).

Bob listed these as an endangered species in the '70s, and he hoped DNA could link this population of wolves to those animals being bred in captivity in New Mexico, thereby strengthening the bloodline. If the blood test matched, it could hopefully prevent the extinction of yet another wolf subspecies. Bob's research, however, posed a threat to local trappers in the region. If these wolves were in fact red wolves, an endangered species, and not gray wolves as previously assumed to be, then all trapping in that region would be curtailed while a lengthy research was conducted to further examine the status of these animals.

The trapping community on Prince of Wales Island was not going to just stand by and let some college boy interfere with their livelihood. I flew into the small airport on Prince of Whales where Bob met me and another volunteer, Sean. We would be assisting in trapping and fitting archipelago wolves with radio collars. There had been some setbacks in his research, and the troubled expression on Bob's face told us that all was not well in paradise. Some local boys, it seemed, had honed in on Bob's radio frequency and were tracking down and killing the radio-collared animals in defiance to his research.

Since these wolves traveled in packs, the entire resident populations were being affected. One pack of nine animals had already been completely annihilated. This was a very real threat to Bob's project, and we were anxious to help wherever possible. The densely wooded island was part of the Tongass National Forest and encompassed a staggering 17 million acres of land in Southeast Alaska. The massive spruce trees were a valuable resource for the residents here, and the economy revolved around the production of lumber. If you weren't a fisherman on Prince of Wales Island, you were probably a logger.

The giant Sitka spruce towered high into the air, blocking most of the sunlight from reaching the forest floor. This was truly a magical place. In addition to the wolves, there were Sitka blacktail deer, black bear, a few brown bears, and numerous other mammals living on the island. Majestic bald eagles were common, especially along the coastline. Eagles were typically perched high in the trees, enabling them to scan the pristine waterways for spawning salmon. Bob pointed out a massive nest atop an old snag. The nest was more than eight feet across and would probably top out at close to a ton.

I pulled my binoculars from my duffel bag to have a closer look at the mammoth structure. Two small eaglets could be seen peering over the lip of the nest. The adult eagles added new branches every year, Bob told us. The weight already being exerted on the old snag appeared to exceed what the withered spruce could bear. The tree was listing seaward, and one good wind would probably topple the ancient giant.

"She probably won't make it through the winter," Bob guessed.

But the rapidly growing chicks would be testing their wings by month's end. I could only hope his prediction was true. We traveled deeper into the forest, following old logging roads.

"Without these roads," Bob said, "the wolves would already be protected from exploitation. The trees here were too dense for snow mobiles, so logging roads were the only human access."

"What about boats?" I asked.

"The coastline is too rugged," he answered. "Those rocks would demolish a boat in minutes."

We entered a large clear-cut. The tangle of fallen timber littered the ground.

"They only take the biggest trees," Bob informed us. "The rest are left to rot." There was a distinct note of sadness in his voice.

"It will take at least fifty years for these trees to grow back."

When flying in, I witnessed the devastation firsthand, and it was heart wrenching to see the huge swaths of forest laid to waste.

"They log this area the same way they fish," he said. "Take a little, kill a lot. Such a terrible waste."

From what I had seen both in the air and now in the forest, I would have to agree. We traveled for another forty minutes or so and at last reached the crudely constructed camp. When I exited the truck and stepped to the forest floor, the silence was deafening. The thick covering of damp moss and spruce needles encased the fallen branches, boulders, and logs in what resembled a blanket of an emerald green snow.

"It rains a lot here," Bob announced. "I hope you boys brought rain gear."

"That's all I brought," I replied. "Even my jockey shorts are coated in Teflon." I hoped the humor would help lift his morose spirits.

The literature I had researched prior to my arrival indicated this was a temperate rainforest. Up to three hundred inches of rainfall fell a year. Even now, a persistent drizzle of moisture was trickling through the dense canopy. We carried our gear into camp where three large canvas tents had been constructed in a small clearing. There was also a small wooden building tucked into the trees a short distance away. There was a lock on the door and a sign Keep Out in bold red letters.

"Is that where you keep your tracking equipment?" I asked.

"No, that's a decoy," he replied. "It's actually the outhouse." A smile lit up his face. "I've been vandalized three times," he said, shaking his head. "By the time they pry the lock off the door, they'll sadly discover they broke into the dunny. They usually give up. I keep all the valuables locked in the truck." Bob told us, "Otherwise I would already be out of business."

We stashed our gear in an empty tent and ducked through the doorway of the cook tent. The kitchen area consisted of a two-burner stove and a large white cooler to store anything perishable. There was also a table constructed of a four-by-eight sheet of one-inch plywood with two planks stacked on five-gallon water barrels to provide seating. Boxes of canned goods were neatly piled on wooden pallets to keep them off the damp floor of the tent.

"Peas, green beans, pinto beans, chili beans, even lima beans," I read. "Don't they sell anything but beans here?" I asked. "The wolves will know I'm coming before I leave the tent."

"They'll know anyway," he said. "A wolf has thirty thousand scent receptors in its nose. They can smell this camp from a mile away."

We sat down for lunch after the groceries had all been stowed. We spread canned sockeye salmon on saltines with sliced cheese and the "fiesta resistance" locally grown raw oysters. The cold, clear ocean water entering the bay was ideal for growing the shellfish. I had never eaten oysters raw; but after getting used to the slimy texture, the flavor was delicious, and you couldn't find fresher seafood anywhere.

In the following few weeks, I would learn more about the art of tracking, trapping, and identifying animal signs than I could have ever imagined. Bob, it turned out, was a master woodsman. He grew up in the remote, temperate forests of Washington State and knew the woods and its inhabitants intimately. As a boy, he trapped to make extra money but lost interest when he once set up a lynx trap. It accidentally snapped shut on his right hand, breaking three fingers and partially severing one. Deciding he would no longer subject wild animals to the incredible pain and suffering they endured when captured in this fashion, Bob opted instead to use his talents to save rather than destroy the wildlife he had grown to love.

"Besides," he said, "why would intelligent women of fashion go to such great lengths to pluck, wax, and shave all the unwanted hair from their bodies just to cover it all up with the fur of a different species?"

People who often wear furs are usually so far removed from the natural world. Only recently were they made aware of the torture these animals undergo to provide the furs. Women typically wear furs not to survive the elements but to flaunt their wealth. I am thankful the U.S. market for furs has greatly diminished. Sadly, Europeans have not yet learned if humans were meant to wear fur, we would grow our own.

To get close to the wolves, we were first instructed on how to eliminate human scent from our clothing. By boiling everything in spruce needles, you smelled more like a bottle of Pinesol than a box of Tide. The clothing was then line dried while wearing rubber gloves. Since nothing here ever completely dried, you had to get used to wearing cold, damp clothing whenever you were in the field. Our rubber boots were painted with a pungent concoction of castor oil extracted from the scent glands of beavers and mixed with pine sap. Something told me I would be donating my wardrobe to the camp when my volunteer work here was completed. Even here in Southeast Alaska, the airlines had rules about personal hygiene before boarding. So to be safe, I set aside some clothing for the day of departure.

The following morning, Bob instructed us on setting the padded traps used to capture the wolves. A single fingerprint would be detected by the animals, so rubber gloves were worn at all times. Everything, including the bait, could not be touched without a glove, or the trap would be rendered useless. It was at this point our companion, Sean, announced to us that he would be unable to assist in the trapping process. He apologized profusely but stated he loved wolves too much to catch them in traps. He would, however, gladly remain in camp and help in any other ways.

"I can cook," he volunteered.

I thought Bob would be furious at the man for quitting so soon; but in a calm, controlled voice, he graciously accepted help in the kitchen department.

He turned to me and asked, "You okay with this?"

"Sure," I answered.

I was concealing my true feelings on trapping even in the name of science. I had seen animals in leghold traps in Arizona. It seemed a cruel and barbaric practice, so

I vowed to destroy any traps I encountered after discovering an emaciated kit fox caught and left to starve in a leghold trap outside of Tucson.

These traps were padded to lessen the possibility of serious injury to the animal. The sensors had been installed to signal when the trap was sprung, thereby minimizing the length of time the animal was held. Still I wished there was another way. But all things considered, I would give it a try, hoping the research would eventually protect the wolves we were hoping to capture. So off we went, single file in search of the elusive archipelago wolf.

Island Wolves Final Chapter

A S WE ENTERED the forest, the maze of game trails crisscrossed in all directions. I wondered how Bob knew if he was going in the right direction.

"Do you ever get lost out here?" I asked. I hoped the experienced woodsman wouldn't find my inquiry offensive.

"We're lost now," he replied. "But we're making good time."

The cloud cover made it impossible to get a bearing on the direction of the sun.

"How do you find your way in these woods? Just in case we get separated."

He produced a small devise from his coat pocket about the size of a cell phone.

"GPS." He handed me the small instrument. "Never leave camp without it. Better stick close, but if you do get lost, just don't wander off. I'll come back and find you before dark."

There were a million questions bouncing around in my head, but I was uncertain how soon we might be in earshot of wolves, so my questions would have to wait.

We stopped every so often to examine a plant or look at a faint track visible in the occasional patch of exposed earth. A huge mushroom growing on the side of a rotting stump caught my attention.

"Psst, what's that one called?"

"Chicken of the woods."

"Edible?" I stroked the giant fungi with my finger.

"You have to get a young one." He pointed to a shelf under a rock ledge.

"There are a lot of mushrooms in the Tongass," he said. "But only a few are good to eat. Angel wings and shaggy manes are the easiest to identify, but if you're not sure, don't experiment."

We entered a small clearing.

"These can kill you," he said, pointing to a patch of dome-shaped bright orange mushrooms about the size of a tennis ball.

A small mammal scurried up a nearby tree, launched itself into the air, and glided gracefully to an adjacent one.

"I thought flying squirrels lived in the South," I said as I watched the rodent disappear into the canopy.

There was no reply. Bob stopped. He raised his right-hand palm open, then closed it to a fist. I recognized the military hand signal to freeze. Dropping to one knee, I awaited further instructions. Something or someone had sprung a trap. The flashing light on the sensor told Bob which of the traps was indicating a capture.

"Wolf?" I asked. Excitement was mounting in my voice.

"Might be anything." He checked the GPS.

"Pine martens trigger a lot of them."

The pine marten is an arboreal member of the weasel family. Their diet consisted primarily of rodents and birds. The spruce hen, a slow-witted member of the grouse family, was the marten's favorite prey. Although they were efficient hunters, the martens were not opposed to raiding a trap, and they were usually clever enough to release the prize and escape.

"What else do you catch?"

We set off again in a southerly direction. In my vivid imagination, I pictured a ten-foot-tall grizzly with a number 4 wolf trap dangling from his paw and he was waiting for the damn fool who set the thing to show up and take it off his tender paw.

Bob apparently read my mind and answered my question that I hadn't actually asked.

"Bears sometimes get caught. But unless it's a cub, they usually walk right out of it. We should know any moment now."

We entered another clearing. In the center, there was a small pond and a beaver dam some thirty feet in diameter. If a wolf could catch a beaver away from the safety of its lodge, it would make a great meal. I knew beavers were the largest rodents in North America, and a large male could weigh up to forty pounds. That would be a feast, I thought. The alder trees and willows at the water's edge were cut and peeled recently, indicating the lodge was occupied.

"The wolves patrol this area fairly often," Bob commented while scanning the opposite bank. "I set one of the traps in that brush piles in hopes of getting their attention on their next pass through here."

There was rustling in the dense brush where Bob had pointed. The trap was set. Something had been caught in the trap, but until we crossed to the opposite side of the bog, we wouldn't know what it was.

The Island Wolves Captured

Kenai A beautiful gray wolf raised at Cougar Hill Ranch

T HERE WAS NO quiet way to cross the marshy bog. Our boots sank halfway up the shin in the quagmire and with every step; black ooze gripped the neoprene, threatening to suck the waders from our feet. After crossing the small stream that fed the beaver pond, the mud gave way to the sphagnum moss. Every few steps, tiny insectivorous plants called Venus flytraps could be observed lying in wait for the buzzing insects.

If you were not eating something out here, something was probably eating you.

The movement in the bushes had suddenly ceased. Bob quickly assembled his jab pole (a device that holds a syringe loaded with a sedative), and in this case, it was ketamine. Ketamine is used to temporarily immobilize the wolves so they can be safely examined and the radio collars fitted and secured around the neck. By standing on top of a fallen tree, I was at last able to peer into the dense foliage. The dark brown fur accompanied with the throaty whine identified the creature being held securely in the trap.

A beaver, apparently while cutting tender willow for its winter larder, had stumbled into the open jaws of the trap. Now beavers might be nothing more than an overgrown hamster, but this big hamster had three-inch incisors. Those teeth were capable of chiseling through a grown tree in minutes, so we cautiously debated how best to release the annoyed rodent and still keep all our fingers and toes.

"Can you dart her?" I asked.

"I could, but it may take hours for the anesthetic to wear off. If she goes in the water too soon, she could drown." He stepped forward cautiously. "I have a better idea. Try to get a hold of her tail and lift her off the ground. I should be able to remove the trap without too much difficulty."

"For a college-educated man and a biologist to boot," I said, "you sure come up with some crazy ideas. The way I see it, from the tip of the beaver's tail to the tip of those very large teeth is about three feet."

"Your point?" he said, waiting to hear the significance of my approximation of a beaver's length.

"Well, that's about the exact same distance from my hands to my groin. I was circumcised at birth. I didn't really enjoy it then and would not particularly care to repeat the process now. How about if we throw a coat over the animal? I can hold her down, and you get your trap back."

Bob nodded his head in agreement and, removing his jacket, approached the angry rodent matador-style. Not realizing we were here to help, the beaver lowered her head and prepared for battle by emitting a loud guttural warning. We would prevail, I assured myself, but this wasn't going to be a walk in the park. Instead of backing away from her tormentor as I expected, the beaver lunged forward. Her webbed foot slipped from the padded jaws of the wolf trap, but not realizing she was free, she continued with the attack. Bob threw the coat over the advancing mammal, but in an instant, the coat with beaver inside it was wrapped around Bob's ankles. Jumping into the air, first one foot and then the other, the surprised trapper reminded me of a barefoot Boy Scout who just stumbled into the campfire. Leaping backward, Bob couldn't understand how the beaver was able to stay on top of him.

"She's loose," I shouted.

I was able to warn Bob of his precarious situation just about the time the ferocious beast shot out from under the jacket. With jaws snapping, the angry rodent chased the fleeing man across the meadow. Bob was staying about one step ahead of the fur-bearing chain saw when suddenly, she veered off and dashed headfirst into the pond. Slapping the water with her large flat tail, the beaver disappeared beneath the surface of the water. Bob, in his usual carefree manner, looked first at the pond then back at me, still perched on the fallen log.

"Well, that was fun. Whaddaya say we radio-collar some beavers when we're finished with the wolves?"

A smile extended from ear to ear. "We're going to need steel-toed boots for these guys," I said, pointing at the three-inch laceration in the toe of his rubber waders.

"That's about as close as I want to come to a beaver pedicure. Let's reset the trap a little farther from the pond," he suggested, "and call it a day."

We laughed all the way back to camp. Sean was waiting anxiously to hear about our great adventure, and an adventure it was indeed. It would be several more days before we would finally capture a wolf, but our close encounter with the beautiful, bold beaver would not be soon forgotten. That day, I gained an even deeper appreciation for these marvelous architects and their tenacious ability to do battle.

Departing the Archipelago

I CAN'T SAY for certain what day of the week it was when the flashing light on the sensors indicated a trap had been sprung. On two previous occasions, we had rushed out to the secluded location only to find an empty trap. Once, a pine marten had stolen the bait; and the second time, a fallen branch had tripped the device.

At camp, I picked Bob's brain for everything pertaining to the Tongass National Forest and the creatures that resided here. He would patiently answer my every question, but when it came to wolves, there was a passion in his voice. This indicated to me these animals were more than just another carnivore. Saving the wolf had become his purpose in life. Quite possibly, no one knew more about wolves of the archipelago than he did, not even the hunters that sought to destroy them.

"Their diet," he said, "is mostly ungulates. The small Sitka blacktail deer is their primary food source, and once again this puts them into direct competition with man."

The human residents of this island hunted these deer, which were no larger than a Great Dane. Bob created a recipe for the tasty venison that he referred to as Sitka stew, which could be made of 80 percent venison and 20 percent carrots with a helping of celery, potatoes, and cabbage thrown in if available. The concoction was then seasoned with lots of pepper to mask the gamelike odor of the meat, and voilà.

The wolves, of course, hunted other animals as well. Beavers, birds, voles, even spawning salmon were part of their diet. Large packs of wolves were even capable of dispatching a black bear but usually not without causalities. These powerful bruins were equipped with claws. Bears wouldn't hesitate to lash out with their razor-sharp weapons, which are primarily used for scurrying up the trees, that could inflict crippling wounds on their attackers.

I was following the coordinates on my GPS unit. As the audible beeping got stronger, I knew we were closing in on the trap. Bob stopped to examine the fresh scat partially buried in the peat moss. The undigested deer hair was indisputable proof that this was wolf sign. Twenty yards ahead, his suspicion was confirmed. The gray and brown head of an adult archipelago wolf appeared above the brush. Other wolves could be seen fleeing toward the trees. Unwilling to abandon their captured comrade, the remainder of the pack stared back at us from the safety of tree line. These wolves had all the characteristics of their much larger cousins. But the coloration was unlike that of any wolves I had ever seen. A light tan undercoat covered with long black-tipped guard hairs served to repel moisture. Typical mainland wolves were gray or sometimes black.

The trapped wolf put up little struggle and, unlike the beaver, displayed no signs of aggression. Rolling on his back in a submissive posture, the timid animal lay quietly, awaiting his fate.

How could anyone, I wondered, seeing this beautiful creature lying helplessly in the trap club it to death for its pelt? Bob was quickly assembling the pole, while I drew the ketamine into the syringe. Checking the dosage, he plunged the needle into the flank of the quivering animal; and in a few moments, its muscles began to relax. I was speechless. I was now standing inches away from this legendary animal, and I began to reflect on my own misconceptions about the wolf.

Why, when faced with certain doom, would this animal not lash out at its captors? It soon became apparent to me why the descendant of *Canis lupus* would prove to be mankind's most trusted companion. Over ten thousand years ago, possibly my own ancestors would have to rely heavily on these superb predators to aid in their survival. And to repay them for their valuable contribution, mankind nearly wiped them off the face of the earth.

As we removed the trap from the wolf's leg, I made a promise to myself that whenever possible, I would share my knowledge, love, and appreciation of wolves to anyone who would listen. That promise would eventually take me into the classrooms of animal lovers from six years old to sixty. Like my mentor Bob Ballard, I would do my part to pay back the debt we have owed the wolf for more than ten thousand years.

After the blood was drawn to check the DNA, a radio collar was bolted in place, and an injection was administered to counteract the sedative. The pack howled mournfully in the forest, calling to their mate. I ran my fingers through the soft undercoat.

What would the pack make of my strange scent? A scent that until now spelled only death and destruction, so I moved away as the wolf rose to her wobbly legs. Looking back at me one final time, she rejoined her welcoming pack.

Tigers on the Golf Course

IF A SURVEY were to be conducted on the average American's favorite big cat, the overwhelming number one answer would most likely be tigers. I have been fortunate in my lifetime to have known several. The first tiger I had the privilege of working with was a young female Bengal named Puffin. She was named after her standard method of tiger greeting, which she did almost constantly. The chuff or chuffing sound is more or less the method that these cats use to say hello.

I recall as a young boy, visiting the local zoo in the foothills above Salt Lake City where I met Shasta, Shasta was not actually a tiger but a liger. Having a lion for a father and a tiger for a mother, Shasta was a rarity indeed. I still remember the special greeting I would receive when I called her name. I was quite certain she reserved her warm welcome only for me, and that beautiful cat left a lasting impression. I knew, even as a youngster, someday I would run my fingers through the elegant striped coat of a living tiger and feel her warm breath on my cheek.

Richard my brave cousin wrestling a lion cub and losing badly

Puffin came to the school from a private zoo in Colorado. She was hand-raised and bottle-fed, and from the very first day I met her, I felt safe in her presence. Now don't get me wrong. I do not know, nor have I ever condoned keeping wild animals as pets. Only trained experts should attempt to work in direct contact with exotics or, for that matter, any potentially dangerous species.

Pet snakes will and have killed their owners. Even domestic horses can injure an inexperienced handler. I was fortunate to have been taught by the finest animal trainers in the world though I still bear scars to prove the fact that wild animals, although trained, are never really tame.

All of the students at the school had the opportunity to work with a variety of animals. Some preferred the primates. Clyde, the orangutan, appeared in the hit movie *Every Which Way But Loose* that starred Clint Eastwood. It was a favorite. The orangutan's humanlike qualities gave you a false sense of comfort. Something like hanging out with your potbellied Irish uncle with the hairy back.

Other students seemed to be attracted to the bears or the exotic birds. But for me, the big cats were number one on my list. Ricktavi, the sleek spotted leopard, or her brother, Magic, had both grown up around people. Both cats were used to being handled by the staff, so it was not uncommon to find a group of students enjoying their lunch in the leopard exhibit. Ricktavi usually had her head in someone's lap sleeping, so students took turns stroking her velvet soft fur.

Tai Chee A rare and beautiful North Chinese Leopard

Puffin, however, loved to explore. In 1979, the school relocated to Lion Country Safari in Irvine Meadows, California. It was an ideal location for the curious young tiger that wanted to get out in the world. Once I graduated, a few simple jobs came along to get me acquainted with life in the entertainment industry. One such job I will never forget.

It sounded quite simple. A large insurance company was having their annual party. This year it was located in Palm Springs and revolved around a circus theme. A big top tent was erected on a local golf course, and two circus wagons at the entrance would display the big cats. The cats we provided were both exceptional animals. One was an African lion named Dandy Lion and the other was the tiger, Puffin. The contract also called for a performance with a chimpanzee and a short skit with a wrestling bear.

Kona the cougar posing for stills in the movie Sams Spa

Sambuka an amazing and gentle white tiger

I rehearsed the basics of the show at the ranch. Michael, a three-year-old chimp, was used to traveling to schools around Southern California to entertain and enlighten the kids. Most had never seen primates like Michael outside a cage and were fascinated by his intelligence and wonderful personality. Pooh Bear was a two-hundred-pound red phase black bear and was exceptionally gentle, so he was used in wrestling acts.

On the ranch, Pooh was used to demonstrate the incredible strength bears possess and would quickly pin any opponent to the ground in a contest. His dancing skills, however, left much to be desired. We arrived at the golf course early. We needed time to get the various props arranged and rehearse the show on-site. Pooh and Michael were placed in a holding area and would be transferred into the wagons. I backed the one-ton flatbed up to the first wagon and lifted the guillotine door.

Dandy Lion walked in and lay down to continue his nap. Puffin's transfer cage, however, would not be as simple. The door on her cage swung open, but it would be impossible to line up with circus wagon without crashing into the tent. I decided to try a different approach. If I could catch Puffin at the doorway, attach her leash, and jump her up into the circus wagon with a piece of meat, it would be far less complicated. I had no idea. Typically, this well-trained cat would go anywhere you wanted her to, but by now, a fairly large crowd of partially inebriated insurance agents had gathered around the tent. Little did they know the show was about to begin.

Jay, my assistant on this program and fellow trainer, slowly opened the cage door, and Puffin jumped down from the truck. I looped the heavy leash around her neck and secured the clasp.

"Wow, that was easy," I said.

Next we approached the circus wagon, and Jay threw a large hunk of red meat into the cage. The problem was Puffin didn't want to eat just yet; she just wanted to visit. Chuffing away, she lunged toward the closest group of spectators. She expected warm receptions with lots of hugs and kisses, but what transpired was complete and total pandemonium.

The group of insurance salesmen scattered in all directions. Knocking over chairs and tables, it was every man for himself. For Puffin, this meant only one thing. The hunt was on. Jay reached out to grab Puffin's leash at the exact same time as a cart loaded with golfers came over the grassy knoll. Puffin immediately focused her attention on the hooting, hollering, club-swinging men. Dressed in white shirts and khaki shorts, the golfers were amazed to see a tiger wandering around on the fairway. They responded in a logical fashion. They fled.

Now a four-hundred-pound Bengal tiger dragging a one-hundred-and-sixty-pound man picked up speed fairly quickly, especially when pursuing a cart full of terrified golf jockeys. Jay, having missed the leash, decided to slow the running tiger down by becoming a human anchor.

In theory, it sounded like a great plan; but by grabbing me securely around the waist, he succeeded in only two things: one, pulling me to the ground, and two, yanking my trousers down around my knees. Realizing the error of his ways, he promptly released me from his grasp. Puffin galloped forward, dragging me through the wet grass. The maneuver turned my entire outfit into one continuous stripe of golf course green. As the golf cart and its wide-eyed occupants disappeared over the rise, the frisky cat lost interest in the chase and returned to the circus tent where she promptly jumped into the wagon and began devouring her snack.

Most of the employees of the insurance company were delighted by the performance and applauded the antics they had just witnessed. They assumed, I suppose, the entire fiasco was part of the show. Jay temporarily refrained from laughing and located a clean shirt. I retreated to the men's room where I tried to wash most of the grass stains from arms and legs.

The remainder of the program went off without a hitch. Well, almost. Michael, the chimp, climbed to the top of the twenty-foot-tall tent pole and refused to come down. He was eventually lured back to his seat with the entire fruit tray from the lunch buffet. Pooh Bear was a huge hit as well. He eagerly wrestled the largest contender in the crowd. After promptly sweeping the man's legs, Pooh Bear plopped down on the man's heaving chest until he admitted defeat.

The long drive home was filled with laughter, but my grass-stained clothing was not salvageable and was donated to Jay's wardrobe. It would serve as a subtle reminder to practice holding on to a leash with both hands.

I left Gentle Jungle the following year to take a position at Cougar Hill Ranch. But I often think back on the many wonderful animals I knew there, especially my first big cat, the wild and wonderful tiger named Puffin.

Poncho

T HE FAINT MEWING in the dark den box was exciting. This was Sasha's second litter, and we were anxious to get a look at the new jaguar cubs. Her first batch was hand-reared by Liz as these would be. It was always a difficult decision to remove the babies, but once a cub opens its eyes, the first thing it sees is whom it would develop the strongest bond with.

It would be my first experience working with jaguars. Veteran trainers preferred leopards or tigers. Without a doubt, "jags" could be tough. Most other cats were considered less tenacious and easier to back down. Though the tigers, cougars, lions, and leopards were all spectacular in their own right, there was something mysterious and haunting about the jaguar.

At one time, these remarkable predators were North America's largest feline predator. Small populations still existed in the Grand Canyon at the turn of the century, but the occasional predation on livestock drastically reduced their numbers – both here and in Mexico. The pelt trade further threatened the numbers of surviving cats. Today, isolated pockets of jaguars and other wild felines still struggle to survive in Central and South America.

*   *   *

The litter count was a total of three – all males and all in perfect condition. We named the largest one Poncho. The first moment I held the helpless small blind cub in my arms, a bond was formed. The precious bundle of spotted fur worked his way deep in my heart, and I found myself preferring his company over that of my own kind.

Liz, Helena, and Helena's sister Bridget were those most responsible for the daily bottle feedings. I became Poncho's surrogate father. There were warnings from other big-cat trainers that jaguars were not trainable.

"That cat will kill you by the time it's three years old," one highly respected handler said.

"Not this cat," I countered. "This one is special."

The secret of being in control, I felt, was to never allow Poncho to become possessive over his food or toys. Secondly, take him everywhere. There was a small stream behind the ranch. Poncho and I would spend most hot summer days swimming in the deep clear pools. In the mid-1980s, there were few neighbors close by, so early-morning hikes far out into the desert were the norm. On more than one occasion, it would dusk before we returned.

Helena referred to Poncho as "my son"; and indeed, if there was ever a cat that had such a profound impact on my life, it was Poncho.

There was a young lioness, Serena, born on the ranch about the same time as Poncho. The two animals became hard-and-fast friends, and I would frequently take both cats out to exercise. When we traveled a safe distance from the road, I would turn Poncho and Serena loose to romp and play in the open desert. I would often sit in the shade of a Joshua tree with one cat on either side dozing in the warm summer sun. Those precious moments will always be some of my most treasured memories.

Poncho and best friend Serena An African Lioness

*   *   *

A forty-acre Christian retreat opened a few miles from Cougar Hill. The setting was stunning. Giant oak trees stood tall alongside a meandering creek running through the middle of the property. I stopped by one evening to inquire as to the possibility of bringing the cubs to romp on the spacious lawns. Joyce, one of the owners, was just eccentric enough to go along with the plan. So one day a week, I would load the cats into the back of the truck for an afternoon picnic at Paradise Springs.

The guests at Paradise Springs loved the up close and personal introduction to the lion and jaguar cubs. Equally, Poncho and Serena had a fabulous outing interacting with many different people. It became such a popular attraction that some patrons of Paradise Springs would only book future reservations if they could be assured the cats would be there.

A small cabin located on the back lot at Paradise Springs became vacant. Joyce suggested I rent the tiny house for the summer. It was the perfect place to reside.

Poncho would sometimes spend the night in a large dog kennel next to the bed. By six months of age, however, the beautiful young cat outgrew the kennel and the sleepovers were curtailed. The hikes and swims, however, were not. Several hours each day were spent in the company of my two favorite cats. My rapidly diminishing bank account required that I seek gainful employment. A writers strike in Hollywood crippled the movie industry, and trainers everywhere were struggling to stay afloat. A small pub in the local town of Wrightwood had an opening for a bartender, so in spite of the fact that I had never bartended, the owners were impressed that I didn't drink and decided to give me a try.

It was a perfect match. My days could be spent with the four-legged animals, and five nights a week, I became acquainted with a whole new group of animals: the two-legged kind. George, Elizabeth's father, would sometimes stop by for a beer. He usually brought along the cubs or his favorite baboon, Eva. Poncho would hide behind the jukebox and stalk the customers coming in for a cold drink or a quick sandwich. The Raccoon Saloon became the lioness, jaguar, and baboon saloon and a favorite hangout for the townsfolk of Wrightwood.

One day we received a call about a Jaguar car commercial. There weren't a lot of those cats available, so we were hired over the phone. The director had one major concern though. It seemed that previous attempts to use jaguar cats for the commercials resulted in disaster.

"Would Poncho be safe to work with in a studio setting?" he asked.

We invited the director to the ranch to meet Poncho. By the time he arrived, it was midafternoon and time for a swim in the creek. The moment Poncho came into the yard, the man was practically speechless. Poncho was now well over a hundred and fifty pounds, well muscled, and his glossy coat was as shiny as the car he would represent.

"Oh my god!" the man said. "I thought the car was beautiful. This cat is unbelievable. Is it safe to get a little closer?" he asked.

"Sure," I said. "We were planning on going to the creek for a swim. Why don't you join us?"

At first, the man thought we were pulling his leg; but when we handed him the leash and opened the gate, he came to realize how incredibly gentle the cat next to him truly was. Poncho, when meeting a new person, typically wrapped his powerful forearm around the back of their leg and rubbed his large, muscular head on their leg. Understandably, this can be a little unnerving for a first-time introduction, and the director froze in place while the blood drained from his previously flushed cheeks.

"Just pet him," Liz said. "He wouldn't hurt a baby."

Once Poncho realized we were heading for the swimming hole, he quickly lost interest in the man holding the leash and towed him out the gate toward the water. Before leaving that afternoon, the director commented, "This had been one of the most unforgettable afternoons of my life. Is there anything you need to prep the cat for the commercial next week?"

"A deposit would be fine, and if possible, the loan of a Jaguar car so Poncho could get used to the smell and sound of the engine," I laughed.

That statement was a joke of course, but the gentleman wrote out a check for the deposit and, unbeknown to any of us, called his office to have a Jaguar XJ6 delivered to the ranch for one week. I don't know if Poncho got used to the car, but I definitely did. For the next seven days, the tiny town of Littlerock, California, had its fill of the trainers from Cougar Hill Ranch driving up and down its main street in the sixty-thousand-dollar sports car.

The commercial titled *The Cat Is Back* went off without a hitch, and the car was reluctantly returned in the same condition as when it arrived.

Poncho went on to appear in other car commercials but never in a full-length motion picture. He lived to the ripe old age of twenty-two. I received the call at Camelot informing me of Poncho's death. Everyone who shared the privilege of knowing that wonderful cat shed a tear in his passing. No one more than I. There would be only one big cat I would call my son. Each time I look at the framed picture of Poncho above my desk, I reflect on the great joy he brought into my life and how truly blessed I was to have known him.

Mailai and Macurro

IN THE SUMMER of '84, I was offered a job in the nearby town of Rosamond, California. The facility was a private animal compound called Randy Miller's Exotic Wildlife. Randy was a young entrepreneur from Beverly Hills with a passion for exotic cats. His small menagerie of animals consisted of a six-month-old Siberian tiger named Shere Kahn, two black Leopards named Macurro and Mailai, and one out-of-control African lion named Razzle Dazzle. There was also a lovely cougar named Kona and a new baby Siberian lynx lovingly referred to as Kiowa.

The newly formed business venture was seeking a trainer with experience specifically with the big cats. It sounded like an ideal job. To go to work every day and play with tigers and leopards was every naturalist's dream. The bonus was there was a regular paycheck, and I wouldn't have to rely on the movie industry to pay my bills. The downside was I would be leaving my human and animal friends at Cougar Hill Ranch to take the position.

Randy was interested in getting his cats in movies and commercials, and my connections with Cougar Hill Ranch was perceived as a big plus. I met with Randy at his warehouse in Walnut, California, to discuss the terms of my employment; and since it seemed like a good match, I was hired on the spot. The young man in excellent physical condition also had excellent business savvy. He had taken over his grandfather's small street vending business and turned it into a multimillion-dollar industry. What Randy was lacking was a working knowledge of training big cats. That was hopefully where I came in.

I drove to Rosamond the next morning to meet with Nati Alvarado, the current caretaker in charge of feeding and caring for the collection of felines. Nati had previously trained dogs but recognized the fact that training a Labrador to sit and fetch was far different from training a four-hundred-pound tiger to walk on a leash or go to a mark untethered.

The position he held with Randy was not in sync with Nati's long-term goals of training police dogs, but he graciously agreed to stay long enough to get me acquainted with all the cats. I walked down the line of spacious cages and greeted the occupants one by one. Considering that this was a collection of basically wild, untrained big cats, they were all extremely well mannered and quite socialized.

There's no time like the present, I always said, to find out just what you are dealing with; so I unhooked the steel chain from around the first doorway. I slowly opened the gate and attached a leash around the muscular neck of the emerging tiger. Shere Kahn, the eight-month-old cub, wrapped his soup-pot-sized paw around my calf and placed his even larger mouth around my thigh. His large canine teeth pressed forcefully into my flesh, and with that, the spunky young cub got his first lesson in tiger etiquette. A swift, startling punch in the nose sent the cat reeling backward. Nati looked at me with a shocked expression on his face.

"He's just playing when he does that," he said.

"He may be playing now," I responded. "But Shere Kahn only weighs about eighty pounds. Wait till he gets to be about six or seven hundred pounds and he still thinks it's okay to put his mouth around your leg. Setting some boundaries when he's young will help this beautiful animal not have to spend the rest of his life behind bars."

"When you put it like that," Nati said, "it makes sense. You don't really want to be a teething ring for a cat that can someday chew your arm off?"

"Follow the lessons a mother tiger teaches her cubs and you can't go wrong."

I was grateful the cats were still young animals; although they were all very social, every one of them had extremely bad and potentially dangerous habits. Everyone, that is, with the exception of Kona, the cougar. I have always had a fondness for these remarkable predators, but I have met few cougars with such a sweet and gentle disposition as Kona. Not only was he trustworthy, but he was also a remarkably patient and loyal companion. For the next eighteen months, it would be my great pleasure to watch him grow and mature.

Less than six weeks after being hired by Randy Millers Exotic Wildlife, I received a call from Nick at Cougar Hill Ranch.

"How are those two young leopards?" he asked.

"They're great," I said. "Why, do you have a job for them?"

"Mind if I stop by and take a look? I'm right around the corner."

One thing my good friends at Cougar Hill would never have to do is ask permission to come by. They were and are still today as close as any family I have ever had.

"Please do," I said.

When Nick arrived, I took the two cats into the training compound and new obstacle course I had designed. I demonstrated the routines I had been practicing with the cubs, and Nick told me a little bit about the job he was working on. He hoped to have the deal finalized by week's end. *China Beach* was a popular, long-running television series about a military medical unit stationed in Southeast Asia during the Vietnam War. This particular segment titled "After Burner" was the story of an orphaned black leopard brought in from the jungle and temporarily fostered by one of the staff members in the MASH unit. Eventually, the cat would be turned over to a proper rehabilitation center. But for now, the frisky orphan was sharing the nurses' tent with disastrous consequences.

Our biggest hurdle to overcome was that the actress playing the part of nursemaid to the little cat had been previously clawed by her own house cat and was not too keen on tangling with the twenty-five-pound buzz saw we were about to introduce her to. We would have less than two weeks to prepare her in the delicate art of working around wild animals, and from the very start, things were not looking very promising.

We arrived on the set early Monday morning with the two leopard cubs. They were both identical in size and color. While Macurro was more outgoing and bold, Mailai had a sweet, easygoing disposition – as far as leopards go. Both cats would have a part in the film even though they would be portraying the same animal.

When the lead actress arrived, it was apparent she was extremely nervous and unsure. I sat on the ground with Mailai on my lap and tried reassuring the actress that the young leopards, although very rambunctious, were still just cubs. She would come to find out that these youngsters were quite safe to work with if she followed a few basic rules.

"They are still wild animals," I said. "And you never turn your back on either of them."

"I can do that," she assured me. "Anything else?"

"Never get your face too close to their mouth." I detected a slight flushing in her cheeks at the comment.

"What happens if you get too close?" she asked.

"We are a little thin-skinned as a species," I answered. "If you're going to get bit, it's always a good idea to protect the places you don't want scars."

"If you are trying to get me relaxed around your cats," she said, "you're not doing a very good job."

She was right, but there was no use wasting time beating around the bush. These were potentially dangerous animals, and if she thought the house cat she tangled with left some scars, these cubs could definitely put a hurting on you if you weren't careful. I decided the best approach might be to take Mailai for a walk with the woman and see if the actress could relax in a different setting. There was a vacant field behind the set, so we began strolling casually in that direction. Mailai lost interest in her human companions and focused her attention on the grasshoppers and birds flying in and out of the tall dry grass.

Before long, the woman, Jessica, began to relax around the cub. I passed her the leash, and before she could panic, I began asking her about anything and everything not leopard. As we got farther and farther from the set, we talked about the series, the weather, her hobbies, and her favorite actors. Before long, she was completely at ease. Mailai lay down to rest briefly, and Jessica bent over to stroke the shiny black cat. Trying not to incite any additional fears, I stopped her briefly and instructed her to kneel next to the cub rather than tower over her.

"That way," I said, "you have better control of the leash. Control the leash, and you control the leopard."

By the time we returned to the set, Jessica was proudly and confidently walking Mailai in complete control. The next two weeks of rehearsals were, for the most part, unnecessary. By the time we were ready to begin shooting, Jessica was well versed in everything she would need to know while working with the cubs. I would be dressed in army fatigues so as not to stand out and always ready to step in, if necessary.

There were several scenes in the hour-long film involving the cubs. Everyone involved did a phenomenal job, and by the end of the shoot, the two cubs were as comfortable on a Hollywood set as they were at the ranch. The final scene depicted Jessica saying goodbye to the orphan cub that would be going stateside to a zoo. When the once-cat-shy actress knelt down to pet the leopard for the last time, Jessica made what could have been a very costly mistake.

Concentrating on her lines instead of the cub, she allowed the powerful young cat to place both paws on her bent knee and his chin on her shoulder. Before the inevitable happened, I did the only thing I could think of. My acting part was a soldier driving the cat to a waiting plane. I jumped from the jeep with my heart in my throat and walked briskly toward the impending disaster. As I got closer, I realized my heart-stopping panic attack was unwarranted. Jessica's left hand had a firm grip on the leash, and even while quoting her lines and hugging Mailai goodbye, she was in absolutely no danger. The one-time student had graduated with honors as a first-class leopard wrangler.

I scooped Mailai up from the blacktop, spewing my only line in the movie, "I'll take it from here."

I was stuttering so badly it would require a voice-over to cover up my inability to walk and chew gum simultaneously. Jessica gave me a hug as well while we were loading the cats for the long drive home.

"Keep your day job," she said.

It would be one of the best advice I ever received from a truly great actor, but Hollywood was never really my cup of tea. Randy was delighted to have his very first credits in a film, although my employment with Randy Miller's Exotic Wildlife would be short-lived. My two years of raising and training his wonderful collection of cats would long be remembered as another great adventure in my life.

Randy went on to become one of Hollywood's finest cat handlers. Tragically, at the time this chapter in my book is being written, I heard the unfortunate news that while rehearsing an upcoming commercial, a four-year-old brown bear belonging to Randy attacked and killed a trainer and close friend of his. It comes with the job, I suppose. No one really knows why these tragedies occur; but one thing is certain, anytime a human comes into contact with large, potentially dangerous animals from hoof stock to big cats to sharks, there will always be the inherent danger of getting hurt.

When it comes to working with large predators, however, there is the added risk of coming into contact with mammals that have to kill in order to survive. It would be another lesson I would come to experience firsthand, and it would also bring my career as a stunt double to a close. The story of Bear-Bear would haunt me for years to come. The scars, both external and internal, would cause me to question my ability to read and react to the animals that had been such an important part of my life. It would in fact lead me, for the first time, to fear the creatures that were so much a part of me.

A Panther Prey

R ETURNING TO WHAT I
considered my second home, I was
welcomed by the wilds of Alaska. It would be several years before I returned to
California, and I was already missing the big cats – especially Kona, the cougar, a
cat who allowed me to be a part of his wonderful existence. I'll always remember
the long early-morning walks in the desert with my trusting companion running
through the sage – and blackbrush, unencumbered by cages or chains. For that short
amount of time, Kona would experience freedom, as he was born to have, chasing
birds and rabbits and taking in all the sights and sounds that I could never know.
My own senses were dulled by a life of living in captivity.

It never dawned on me that Kona would run away. Looking back, I wondered
why many of the animals I helped to raise didn't simply vanish when the leash was

removed. Perhaps, they too had forgotten what it meant too live free. Sadly, the steel bars and chain links had become the only security they knew.

Kona would look back frequently and call to me if I ducked behind a boulder or a clump of bushes in an attempt to hide. Once I was located, the agile cat would usually pounce on me momentarily, then settle down on my lap like an overgrown tabby purring contentedly until the time came to return home. Why, I wondered, did I continue to walk away from the things that brought me such great joy? Perhaps, it was my own unrelenting urge to wander. That proverbial greener-grass thing – maybe it was actually some built-in defense mode. If I left first, then I wouldn't risk being left or abandoned. Whatever the reason, the behavior would have to change soon if I was to ever complete my own final circle.

After leaving Redoubt Bay and the bears, I returned to visit my friends at Cougar Hill. The timing was perfect. They were preparing for a new job, and they invited me to come along. It would actually turn into a series of great adventures all involving a beautiful and spirited young cat. A sleek and powerful black jaguar named Bear-Bear was being trained for a very specific purpose. *Jungle Book: Mowgli's Story* was about to begin shooting, and Disney was hiring almost every available animal trainer in the industry for a live animal version of the popular previously animated tale. As in the animated version, Mowgli, the jungle boy, lived in the forests of India with a host of wild creatures that either protected him like a child or hunted him like prey. Cougar Hill would provide several of the main characters including Baloo, which was played by none other than my old friend Casey Bear. Two young hyenas, Fonzie and Laverne, and a new and rising star Bear-Bear, the jaguar, would play the part of Bagherra, the black panther.

From the first day I met this elegant cat, one thing became perfectly clear. This was no Poncho. His assertive personality and stubborn demeanor kept everyone on their toes. It wasn't so much he was aggressive, but Bear-Bear was just tenacious. This was a cat that just refused to back down. This was the kind of jaguar I had been warned about while working with Poncho. Bear-Bear was the not-to-be-trusted kind.

As with all high-energy felines, Bear would require lots of exercise. Long walks would be great, but the problem was there were very few places left to explore in the surrounding and rapidly developing desert. The rolling hills, which only a few years earlier were wide-open, were now fenced in mini ranches with horses, dogs, and worst of all, kids. Unlike Poncho's excursions in the excursions in a forest with Joshua trees, Bear would have to remain on a leash. Every animal we encountered, Bear would perceive as prey. On more than one occasion, I would be dragged behind the powerful cat in his attempt to overtake everything from mountain bikers to fleeing dogs.

The one behavior I could never break was the unnerving habit the jaguar had of wrapping his powerful front paw around my calf and forcefully rubbing his brawny head against my leg. By eight months of age, it became almost impossible to release the forceful embrace. When a stranger would first meet Bear, it could be absolutely terrifying.

There were never any outward signs of aggression associated with the unusual greeting, but just the sensation that you were being claimed by this strong young cat would make people crazy. He would decide when it was time to let go.

Bear-Bear did an absolutely phenomenal job on the set of *Jungle Book*, and no one could argue the fact that the ebony panther invoked a certain spooky feeling when you gazed into his emerald green eyes. By the time Disney wrapped up its production of *Jungle Book*, two more jobs were on the table for the new silver screen star.

Bear-Bear's future looked promising. If the cat could retain his apparently good but forceful nature, *Anaconda* would be the jaguar's next film. It would be a simple one-day shoot. The giant snake attacks and kills a panther along a riverbank in the Amazon jungle. The scene would be shot locally at a small lake in Southern California. True to his nature, Bear was fearless. The forty-foot-long replicas of a real anaconda caused him little concern, and he was eager to shred the serpent to pieces if it came within his reach.

Two things began to manifest themselves in the maturing cat while filming *Anaconda*. One was the fact Bear-Bear began to become possessive over items he deemed to be his. Bowling balls placed in his cage to play with, water buckets, and even articles of clothing left within his reach became his possessions. Soon it became more and more difficult to convince Bear to give these items back. This dangerous new behavior was beginning to emerge in the once-docile cat. This was a bad omen when dealing with animals as powerful as jaguars.

The second and even more concerning change was the fact Bear-Bear began to single people out. Not as friends, but more as prey. It was that attitude that made everyone on the ranch wonder and worry about any long-term film work with an animal that could already easily overpower any one of us. The next television movie would make everyone's worst nightmares come true. And Bear-Bear's first victim would never see it coming.

The Attack

Bear-Bear

THE REMAKE OF Disney's classic *Swiss Family Robinson* had been in the making for several years. Unfortunately, the story would never make it as a must-see movie. Titled *The New Swiss Family Robinson,* it starred Jane Seymour, Stacy Keach, and the legendary David Carradine. With such talented actors, I was somewhat surprised the remake would follow the same predictable plot of the first film. A family stranded on a tropical jungle paradise besieged by calamities ranging from bloodthirsty pirates to fierce creatures lurking around every bend. There was, of course, the comedy and romance thrown in the mix, but all in all, somewhat of a disappointment.

Bear-Bear would fall into the category of fierce creatures. A dark and ominous black panther stalking its hapless victim, Stacy Keach, as he hunts for food to feed his wife, Jane Seymour, and their three children.

Being roughly the same size and stature as Mr. Keach, I would perform the stunt double for the actor. While hunting birds, the actor is stalked and later ambushed by Bear-Bear but escapes with his life by jumping into a lake. Bear was perfect for the shot since he loved to chase and he loved to swim. The one thing none of us expected was the unfortunate deep, dark secret Bear-Bear held – he also liked to bite.

The scene called for a grouse-type bird to be stalked and captured by Keach who was, in turn, being stalked by Bear.

As an old friend of Cougar Hill Ranch, Sylvia, who worked with exotics in the past, was down on her luck and was looking for work. She gave up on her hobby when she was seriously injured by one of her own big cats and now enjoyed a new hobby of raising birds. Sylvia and her bird were hired for what should have been a simple and pain-free shot. The decision to hire the ex-animal trainer would ultimately result in a costly and nearly fatal attack that would drastically affect the lives of everyone involved.

When we arrived on the set, Sylvia was already there. We took Bear-Bear out to stretch his legs and get acquainted with the set. When the strange woman who smelled game birds approached, the predatory instinct of the cat caused it to tense up. After a few moments however, the animal seemed to relax around Sylvia, and she was invited to greet the cat.

Wrapping his paw firmly around her leg, Bear greeted the newcomer in his typical fashion. Smelling her clothing intently, he at last let loose of the leg and began looking at the new sights around him in Malibu Creek State Park where the scene was shot. The area looked nothing like the Amazon rainforest; but its proximity and one other attractive feature, a small lake, would work nicely for the water scene. It called for an unrealistic part where the man escapes the pursuing panther by diving in the water. Water, unfortunately, is the one place where jaguars are more at home than they are on land.

All went well for most of the morning shots. I dressed like the actor and went running down the trail, pursued by the savage cat. Nick was on the release while Liz and Helena were responsible for the actual pickup – catching the cat with a rope once the shot was complete. It was one of the few times in Bear-Bear's life where he was actually allowed, even encouraged, to chase people.

By early afternoon, most of the chase scenes were behind us, and it was time to concentrate on the lake shot. If ever there was a time when working with jaguars got dangerous, this was it. Once in the water, the predatory instinct of these powerful cats kicked in. If Bear caught me in the lake and decided to attack in earnest, there would be little my fellow trainers could do to help. This, however, was "the money shot" as they say; and there was no turning back now. There would be no way of really knowing how Bear-Bear would react until we were in the water, and that time was approaching rapidly.

The jaguar was secured to a stout tree on a long solid chain. He immediately lay down in the shade and began grooming his dark shiny coat. Nick instructed everyone to stay away from the resting cat, and we followed the director to the lake to discuss the next and final scene. Helena stayed behind with the cat since the park was open to the public. There was no telling what foolish things park visitors might do if they discovered a jaguar lying in the shade of a cottonwood tree.

Poncho in his golden years always gentle forever loyal

Before we were all assembled along the shore, frantic cries could be heard from the direction of where the jaguar had been secured. The terrifying screams left little doubt in my mind as to what could have happened. Someone ventured too close to Bear, and the cat had attacked. There was no telling who had been grabbed or how we would ever pry them away. The moment we all feared had arrived, so as I ran in the direction of the screams, I prayed we would get there in time.

Helena's face was ghastly white. Her longtime friend was lying on the ground with a two-hundred-pound cat on top of her. The jaguar's long canine teeth were embedded firmly in the woman's leg, just above the knee. Sylvia was pleading for help, but releasing the animal's powerful grip would be next to impossible. I tried flipping the cat on his back, but he only bit down harder. I could hear the distinct sound of breaking bones as Sylvia's femur began to fracture under the two thousand pounds of jaw pressure exerted by this predator. The harder I fought to get the cat to release her, the more he tightened his grip.

Sylvia's leg was now bleeding profusely, and all but one solution appeared to be inevitable. The park ranger arrived and drew his weapon. It became obvious he may have to shoot Bear in order to save the woman's life. This was one decision I hoped I would never have to make. A loud, booming voice roared from behind me. It was Nick.

"Don't shoot that cat!"

Having grown up working with wild animals, Nick was the only person who could get Bear-Bear to release his deadly grip. Time stood still in what seemed like an eternity. Nick, who had lived and worked around dangerous animals since he was just a child, would risk his own life to not only save Sylvia but also the life of Bear.

Straddling the powerful jaguar's shoulders, he grasped the animal's upper lips and dug his fingers into the tender flesh.

"Grab her arms," he said. "When I pull his mouth open, drag her out of his reach."

Sylvia was moaning in agony. Her face was extremely pale, and there was a pool of blood under her partially severed leg. Nick reached below the cat's jaw and wrenched the lower lip down with all his might. Bear-Bear let out a fierce growl that sent shivers down my spine. But inch by inch, the powerful jaws began to spread apart. Suddenly, the cat released his victim's mangled leg, and I yanked Sylvia across the ground well out of reach of the jaguar's bloody jaws. Nick let go of Bear, and the jaws snapped shut with the force of a steel trap. Lunging to the end of the chain, Bear attempted to reach his prey again, which allowed Nick time to step away from the cat. Instead of backing off, Nick instead grabbed the chain tied around the tree and led the cat forcefully back to the safety of the truck and away from the ranger's loaded gun.

The two veteran animal trainers loaded the angry jaguar back into the cage without incident while first aid was applied to Sylvia's badly damaged leg. A Life Flight helicopter was called in to rush her to the hospital.

"Tell Helena I'm sorry," Sylvia repeated over and over. "I should have never gone up to Bear like that. Tell everyone how sorry I am."

A dozen surgeries later, Sylvia would regain her full use of her leg. We went to visit her while she was in the hospital the day after the attack. Although in intense pain, her first concern was that Bear-Bear was okay. Jane Seymour also paid a visit to Sylvia's hospital room to wish the injured trainer a speedy recovery. On day 3, a lawyer stopped by to try and convince Cougar Hill's longtime friend to file a lawsuit for damages. He succeeded, and a week after the tragic accident, Walt Disney Company and Cougar Hill Ranch were notified of the nine-million-dollar claim.

Sylvia settled for an undisclosed amount of money. The betrayal of the closest friends she had ever known would forever sever her ties with the people who stood by her through thick and thin. Helena, more than anyone, felt responsible for the devastating attack and was brokenhearted over Sylvia's decision to sue the ranch. A month passed by before we heard back from the production company. There was a movie to finish, and the scene in the lake was waiting to be shot as much as we wished this whole nightmare was over. The following week, we would all reconvene at Malibu State Park for the final chapter of *The New Swiss Family Robinson* and my hopeful escape from the jaws of big black jaguar called Bear.

The Final Stunt

THE DRIVE TO Malibu should have been a joyous occasion, but it was the final scene to a movie already fraught with tragedy. Rumors spread of previous injuries with the alligator prior to the attack on Sylvia. To discuss the possibility of yet another incident would bring us all bad luck. We could only hope for the best.

Traffic on the Antelope Valley Freeway was bumper-to-bumper even at this predawn hour. Bear-Bear was loaded into the truck, willing and eager. I avoided any roughhousing with the cat, hoping to keep him calm and relaxed. No use inciting a riot before we had even arrived. Helena appeared overly anxious, but all of us wanted this final shot just to be over with. No one more than me.

"You look tired," Nick said.

It was true. I hadn't gotten a full night's sleep in over a week. The nightmare played over and over in my head. Every agonizing scream, every gruesome detail. What bothered me the most was not reliving the attack itself, but the what-ifs. I remembered all those long walks with Bear-Bear in the desert without ever having a backup. If Bear-Bear had decided to challenge me, then it would have been a definite possibility I could have been killed and the cat destroyed. There was certainly opportunity.

While shooting *Jungle Book*, the jaguar was in close contact with not only the people working on the set but also countless other animals. It was all so unexpected. Or was it? Perhaps we all just wanted to believe he would grow out of his bully stage. Looking back, I now have a much better understanding on how wild animals and domestic pets differ. The difference is remorse.

When Fido decides to chew up your favorite shoes, he has a definite guilty look when reprimanded. Wild animals, however, look at the world in a different light. If something goes wrong, it's the human's fault for not paying closer attention.

Bear-Bear had warned Sylvia to keep her distance. Had we taken the time to look for the obvious signs, the mauling could probably have been avoided. But that was water under the bridge. The nervous energy I was projecting at that very moment could definitely send the wrong signal to Bear. But the mounting anxiety just wouldn't go away. Neither would this shot.

When we arrived, the camera crew was already in place. The best angle for the shot was on a small island in the middle of the lake. The second-unit director approached apprehensively.

"How's Bear feeling this morning?" he asked.

"Seems to be doing fine," Nick answered.

"You ready to do this thing?" he said, looking directly at me.

"Sure," I said, still trying to convince myself the attack on Sylvia was an isolated incident.

I was directed toward the wardrobe to change into the matching attire of the actor I would be doubling. The moment I exited the trailer, there was the distinct feeling I was being watched. Not so much like a shoplifter in a jewelry store, more like the guy named Grave Digger who drew the bull at the rodeo. You know the bull that put four riders in the hospital and flung the clown hiding in the barrel into the next county. Yes, him.

Short and sweet, I told myself. *One take and we will be out of here. Let's get this over with.* Liz was stationed with the camera crew. Once Bear lost track of me, he may head over to the island to investigate something else. Hopefully, I could dive underneath the cat, and he would follow me back to the shore where Nick would be waiting.

We walked through the shot one final time, and we were finally ready. I looked back to Nick for a thumbs-up and caught sight of the piercing green eyes staring in my direction. Bear-Bear's entire focus was directed toward me. A few yards behind the cat, I caught sight of a vehicle, which I would just as soon not have known was there.

The large all-white box with the double doors and two red crosses coupled with the emergency lights on top also stared at me. Before the cold shiver running down my spine could settle in the pit of my stomach, the loud booming voice of the director echoed across the small muddy lake.

"Quiet on the set," he announced, which was totally unnecessary since there were few people not already locked up inside their vehicles and were hardly breathing.

"Roll camera." The faint whirring sound of the camera kicked in. "Action."

Practicing a leopard attack scene with Maccuro

Before Nick released the chain, Bear-Bear was already lunging in my direction. I don't actually really remember running, but since the lake was definitely getting closer, I could only assume I was moving toward the water and not the lake sneaking up on me. I could hear Bear's footsteps getting closer as I leapt into the cold, deep water. Mark Spitz would have been proud at the speed in which I was swimming when I resurfaced. I was perhaps four, maybe five strokes out in the lake, when a loud splash erupted in the water a few yards behind me. When I looked back, the cat was gaining on me quickly.

Three more strokes and I took a deep dive below the surface. If I could hold my breath long enough, I would be halfway back to the shore before the jaguar knew which direction I had gone. When I opened my eyes underwater and looked skyward, I could faintly make out the outline of Bear swimming in circles above me. One thing was certain, he wasn't giving up on the chance at another victim just yet.

My lungs were all but bursting when I resurfaced. Nick was standing at the water's edge with a big smile on his face. The shot was perfect. Bear had arched high in the air and in hot pursuit. It was such a believable chase scene, and the director was ecstatic as well. Desperately trying to get away from the cat was truly authentic – little did they know.

While Nick secured Bear, someone handed me a towel to dry off. Everyone was apparently satisfied with the shot we had all been dreading, but then came the bad news.

That old adage "Anything that can go wrong, will go wrong" always happens at the worst possible time. The director walked in my direction, shaking his head.

"We have to do it again," he said.

If this was some sort of practical joke, the timing was all wrong.

"Are you serious?" I asked. "Why?"

"They didn't get it."

"Who didn't get it? I looked back at Nick shaking his head.

"The camera man ran out of film at the last minute," the director said. "We have to do it again."

This was the first and only time I had ever wanted to quit on a movie. Things happen. The actor forgets his lines, the animal goes in the wrong direction, etc. They actually made a show about such things called *Blunders and Bloopers*. Usually, it's understandable, but not this time. Never does a camera just run out of film, especially not at a time like this.

There was no getting around it. I headed back to the wardrobe for a change of clothing for take 2. This time, however, we would be dealing with a wiser, more determined cat. We wouldn't be fooling Bear-Bear a second time. For him, the game had just gotten dangerously predictable.

When I returned to the set, I was still shivering. I would like to think it was the ice-cold lake, but in July, the lakes in Southern California typically don't get much below lukewarm. My knocking knees and I knew it had little to do with the water temperature and a lot to do with the bone-crushing jaws of a very intense black jaguar.

This wasn't going to get better with time like a good bottle of Merlot. I was going back in the water, and Bear-Bear was more determined than ever.

"Last time," I said, looking back at Nick.

"Ready on the set," called the director. "Roll camera and action."

This time, I do remember running. I wasn't looking back this time either. If Bear had any intentions of catching up with this cowboy, he'd better be able to fly. Fortunately, the cat preferred going high, instead of going long. By the time Bear hit the water, I was halfway to the island. Instead of continuing the pursuit, he actually gave up on the chase and swam back to the shore.

There was enough good footage in the two takes to call the shot a wrap, and as far as I knew, *The New Swiss Family Robinson* was a done deal. Bear was lying on the bank, licking his wet fur and paid little attention to any of us. A boat took the director over to the island to review the tape, and after a few minutes of peering into the camera, he looked over with a big smile and gave us a thumbs-up.

Liz came back in the boat, and we began gathering up the various props to load into the truck and head home.

"The second jump in the water was even better than the first," she said.

"How did I look?" I asked.

"Scared," she answered with a laugh.

Nick was still talking with the director, who was setting up for the next shot. I could tell he wasn't entirely happy about the topic being discussed. He waved us over to inform us the director had requested one additional shot of Bear chasing me down a trail. This was a bad idea for a variety of reasons. The animal is fixated on me, the target, and it was now no longer a game. Secondly, something changed the moment the jaguar entered the water. He became predaceous. Nick suggested we take Bear for a walk to see how he would react to me outside the water. Against all instinct, I reluctantly agreed.

It would be a decision I would live to regret and would bring an end to my career working with big cats or, for that matter, all large predators. Initially, the jaguar paid little attention to me. We walked along the trail where the final scene would be filmed. I stayed well out of reach of the cat's powerful grip. We all knew Bear would eventually be running loose during the shot, and I would have nowhere to hide.

"Let him come up and say hi," Nick said.

Everything inside me said this was a bad idea, but as the cat got nearer, I began to relax.

This was Bear-Bear, I told myself. I had known this animal since he was a cub. Whatever happened with Sylvia had nothing to do with the relationship we shared. Bear rubbed his big powerful head along my leg while I reached down to give the cat a firm pat. As usual, he wrapped his still-wet paw firmly around my leg.

"Leave it," I said. But before the command escaped my lips, I knew I was in trouble. His grip tightened, and a deep growl rumbled from within his chest.

"Leave it," I repeated as the vivid recollection of Sylvia, lying on the ground in a pool of her own blood, flashed through my mind.

Like falling off a bridge, everything began to happen in slow motion. The mouth of the fixated cat opened wide, exposing the deadly canine teeth. I saw more than felt them sinking into my flesh.

"He's got me, Nick," I said. My heart was racing.

"No, he doesn't," he said. I looked down at the powerful jaws spread wide and the massive ivory white canine teeth clamped down on my lower leg. Instinctively I dropped to the ground and delivered a solid kick to Bear's face with my free leg. Bear bit down harder, his teeth grinding their way to the bone. Once more, Nick risked his own life by straddling the jaguar's front legs and grasping both the upper and lower jaws. Wrenching open the animal's mouth just wide enough allowed me to free my bloody leg. The words from his quivering voice expressed his feelings of deep remorse for putting me in harm's way.

"You saved my life, Nick," I said. "We all know the risks involved every time an animal comes out of the cage."

I stood up, testing my leg while Nick and Liz returned Bear-Bear to his cage. There was surprisingly little pain, and the speed in which Nick reacted didn't allow time for the cat to fracture the bone. I could feel the warm blood oozing down my calf, and as I hobbled toward the waiting ambulance, I remembered passing a woman holding the hand of a small child. They had witnessed the attack from the other side of a barrier fence, which had been erected while we finished the last scene.

"What happened to your leg?" the girl asked. She was perhaps nine or ten years of age, and I didn't wish to frighten her.

"We are filming a movie," I said. "This is fake blood they put on to make it scary." The mother looked down at the gaping hole in my pants and probably figured out the wound in my leg was not special effects. As I climbed into the back of the waiting ambulance, I looked back and smiled my most convincing smile to the mother and daughter.

"What happened?" the driver asked.

"I'm going to need a few stitches," I said. As he cut away the soaked pant leg and began digging around for a gauze bandage, he looked more closely at my injured leg.

"You're going to need more than that," he said. "That's a nasty bite."

As we headed toward the hospital, a deep throbbing ache began to settle into my lower leg.

"How did you get into this line of work?" the attendant asked.

"It's a very long story," I said. "It started when I was just seven years old, and it has been the best life I could ever have imagined."

By early the next morning, I was checking out of the hospital and was waiting for a ride back to the ranch. Liz and Helena picked me up in the old forest green pickup, and we jumped on Interstate 5, heading east.

"How's your leg?" Nellie asked.

"Good as new," I answered. "How's Nick?"

"He's feeling pretty bad about you getting hurt. He blames himself."

"It was my decision to let Bear come up to me, and no one is to blame. It just happened."

We would try one more time to take Bear-Bear on a walk, but there was little doubt in anyone's mind if he could have reached me, he would finish the attack he started on the set. Bear-Bear would retire from the business, as would I. It had been a good run with happier memories than I could count.

But as they say, "It was time to hang up my spurs." As I drove back to Moab later that week, I looked to beginning construction on my new Camelot Lodge. I had no idea within a couple of years I would be back in front of the camera lens, walking a new young animal actor in her first debut. Kika is a cougar who starred in her first role as a powerful predator in the BBC wildlife documentary called *Wild New World*.

Living and working with animals was all I had ever known, and maybe, I wasn't ready to throw in the towel just yet. Maybe, it was just time for a whole new adventure.

The Quest for Paradise

A T LAST, THE time had come to take what knowledge I had accrued over the years and start my own business. Although my meager savings might not buy much, with a lot of hard work, it may be enough to at least get me started.

The long winter gave me ample time to put together a business plan for my new lodge. First and foremost was choosing the location. Having spent most of my adult life in the desert, I would write my next chapter of adventures somewhere in the great southwest. I began by looking over maps of Arizona, Nevada, New Mexico, and Utah. Somewhere out there, I would find the perfect home.

There was an unexplained force that kept pulling me in the direction of Utah. It was the place of my birth, and what few happy childhood memories I had were spent there. The desert regions of southern Utah are, without a doubt, some of the most scenic and rugged places in the United States. Millions of acres of state and federal land have been protected from development throughout Utah. Most of the state's most famous national parks are located in its southern portion.

I flew into Salt Lake City shortly after New Year's Day. I called the only family member still residing in Utah; my nephew Steven was as always my pride and joy. Raised without a father, everything this fine man had accomplished in life, he did on his own. With little more than a high school education, it was Steven's incredible work ethics and dedication to his own family that brought about the success in his life. At the age of thirty-three, he was now happily married with a baby on the way. Life for Steven Moore was the best it had ever been.

We visited for a few days. His wife, Ruth, was warm and very welcoming; and she was the light of his life. I told him about my dream of building a guest lodge in the southern part of the state. He had only one suggestion, Moab.

"Home to two world-class destinations," he said. "Arches and the equally spectacular Canyonlands National Park."

It was a great suggestion, but in spite of his advice to travel southeast, I began my search on the opposite side of the state. By ruling out all the other areas I wanted to explore, I could compare Moab and its national parks to Zion National Park, Capitol Reef National Park, the Kaiparowits Plateau, and the newly formed Grand Staircase-Escalante National Monument.

I only had one shot at this. With limited funds, the choice I made would have to be final. So for once in my life, there would be no flying by the seat of my pants. This was my future, and it would be this very important decision that would spell success or failure.

For three long months, I traveled throughout southern Utah. Every canyon, dirt road, and gully was carefully explored. I visited countless small towns such as Ticaboo, Koosharem, Antimony, and Tropic, looking for real estate agents who might point me in the right direction. I hoped to locate a small isolated parcel of land adjacent to a wilderness area I could call home. But everything I saw was either too expensive, too populated, or just didn't feel right.

Raw land, anywhere within a three-hour drive of a national park, would cost a fortune. So I continued working my way east. Most of my trip involved car camping. The little Honda Civic was cramped, but the front-wheel drive got me into places no one in their right mind would have ventured. Winters, even in the desert, can be brutally cold. On more than one occasion, I woke up in the backseat of my compact car, shivering in my mummy bag. Frequently, I would dream that I was still in Alaska. But by early March, the desert began to come alive.

The first edible greens erupted from the sandy soils in April. Wild rhubarb, thimble-sized onions, and dandelion shoots would make a nice addition to my tasteless store-bought salad. The bulbs of the sego lily, Utah's state flower, were high in starch and grew in profusion in the high desert. These plants could be collected only in a survival situation, so I resisted the urge to harvest them. Many of the plants and berries that sustained the early inhabitants of this region could be found in the blossoming meadows and hillsides throughout southern Utah.

Foraging for my next meal became an exciting part of exploration, and this would lead me to other great discoveries. The Fremont Indians disappeared unexpectedly from this area over a thousand years ago. Why they left or where they vanished remained a highly debated topic, but the telltale signs of their existence were still here.

Petroglyphs and pictographs were painted on the protected rock walls. Images were pecked into the sandstone with primitive tools, and dyes were found in many of the secluded canyons and arroyos. Most, if not all of these ancient images, were located along popular hiking trails. Several had been vandalized and defaced, though, in the more isolated areas; I located entire untouched villages built in stone. These treasures from the past, for the most part, were completely intact.

Next to one cliff dwelling, I discovered an oval granary with corncobs still stored inside. This would be a time of wonderful discovery. Not only would my journey lead me to a deeper insight into the lives of ancient cultures, but it would also be a time to reflect on my own troubled past and the memories that continued to haunt me. The years to follow would be time to forgive and a chance to heal. I couldn't continue blaming my failed relationships or my lack of trust on events that transpired thirty years ago. At least, that was the goal. Only time would tell if I would be able to achieve this long-overdue growth. One thing was certain, however, I might not be able to survive if I didn't.

I was still uncertain as to what attraction my future lodge might have that would attract guests. I knew I wanted it to be different than the motels and bed-and-breakfasts sprouting up throughout the entire southwest. My lodge would be built somewhere secluded. How could anyone truly experience the star-filled desert sky with blaring city lights obscuring them all?

The magic of any wilderness experience, I thought to myself, *is usually a result of and enhanced by the tranquility found there.* This would be one aspect of my lodge that would draw visitors to me. I needed to create a serene and quiet place devoid of the hustle and bustle that often prevailed in any money-hungry tourist town. There would be a unique atmosphere in my new home. It would be a comfortable place where visitors could just relax on a porch swing or explore the backcountry. A place they would feel like a welcome friend when they returned at the end of the day.

I knew about the plants and animals that lived here. Most of my life, thus far, was spent studying wildlife. Hopefully, in time, I could bring a deeper appreciation of the Utah wilderness to my guests. But something was still missing. There was some secret ingredient that would make Camelot Lodge unforgettable. It might be a symbol on a wall, left behind by an ancient, long-departed culture that would show me the answer I was still seeking. But it would be many more months before I would discover it.

Following the Elusive Desert Bighorns

Another member of the bighorn family Dall Sheep from Alaska

I HAVE DISCOVERED few pleasures in life more enjoyable than knowledge. We are indeed blessed in the fact the brave souls who arrived in any given place before us shared their journey. In this way, we too might experience a similar adventure. Hopefully somewhat better prepared and thereby avoiding potential pitfalls.

For me, no voyage is more satisfying than the notion that I am the first one to be somewhere. This place, this species, this miniscule plot of earth was reserved just for me. And the choice to share it with others, or not, depends solely on whether this place or thing satisfies. The human population, now in the billions, leaves little room for personal discovery; but the shrinking world is still full of untouched and unrevealed wonders.

When I awoke, I was enveloped in darkness. The aroma of sweet sage and pinion pine permeated the air. Some faint sliver of light from the crescent moon shone and reflected off the canyon wall. The small pool of water trickled its precious contents into the ravine below.

These hidden springs, located somewhere beneath the Wingate Sandstone, were the lifeblood of the Great Basin Desert. Without water, all living things here would perish. I followed a herd of desert bighorn sheep along a precarious ledge, which dropped more than a thousand feet to the river below. The full-curl ram knew this was a safe haven for the seven ewes and newborn lambs he had sired. The trail led me up a slippery scree slope where I eventually reached a summit. There I discovered two large boulders that formed a gateway. Emerging into an open meadow on the other side was a revelation that would leave me as breathless as the climb itself.

Blackbrush, Indian ricegrass, and several varieties of cacti littered the valley floor. I felt as though I had stepped into a parallel universe. Towering rock walls jutted hundreds of feet into the air, concealing this hidden oasis from the world above and below. A group of inflatable rafts floated lazily around a bend in chocolate brown waters of the Colorado River far below. Their chorus of laughter briefly rebounded skyward. The eerie silence was briefly interrupted by the almost-unperceivable hum of a muffled engine. A long cloud of dust trailing behind the lone Jeep identified its location.

Mankind knew nothing of this hidden valley. The sandstone walls from below appeared unbroken only the jumbled array of hoofprints pointed the way. Curling up in the shadow of a large slab of Cutler sandstone, I began to scour the surrounding cliffs for the elusive bighorns. With the exception of a whiptail lizard darting among the bushes, all signs of life had simply vanished. Even the usually ever-present ravens were nowhere to be seen.

After the strenuous climb following the family of sheep, the thought occurred to me that the secluded meadow, which I had discovered, might be a great place to spend the night. In my backpack was a basic survival kit. A lightweight blanket would keep me warm, and I had an adequate supply of water. My only food consisted of energy bars and beef jerky, which, in this case, would have to suffice for an evening meal. If necessary, the branches of the skunkbrush locally referred to as squawbush were drooping from the weight of ripe berries. The green fruit, although tart, was high in vitamins and, when added to water, produced a drink that resembled the flavor of sugarless lemonade.

Sego lilies were also abundant in the open meadow. I was certain this would classify as a survival situation. So in quasi desperation, I fashioned a digging stick from a pinion branch and filled a small baggie with the nutritious bulbs. As I began to explore the hidden valley, I watched for any footprints indicating the direction in which the animals had fled. A narrow sandy wash running through the center of the valley would be the logical route. Before long, it became apparent my assumption was correct. In addition to the sheep, a host of other wildlife also utilized this corridor as a travel route. Coyote, rabbits, white-footed deer mice, and kangaroo rats had all left their sign. A large snake had also recently slithered across the trail in the general direction of the cliffs.

I frequently encountered gopher snakes in the desert. Sometimes referred to as bull snakes, these harmless constrictors typically displayed little sign of aggression. Occasionally, I would gently pick them up and let them crawl through my hands while I examined them for ticks. These bloodsucking parasites could be easily removed by coating them in Vaseline lip balm.

There were other snakes that also called the Great Basin Desert their home. Lined racers were nearly impossible to capture and were prone to inflicting a nasty bite if mucked with. But it was the faded midget rattlesnake I was careful to watch out for. These meter-long serpents were endowed with powerful hemotoxic venom. The painful bite, if left untreated, could lead to serious complications or even death.

A small rock dislodged from the cliffs above me caught my attention. The family of bighorn sheep that had led me into this magical place was huddled on a small narrow ledge no more than a hundred feet above. The powerful ram was still in the lead, but it appeared he would be unable to proceed much farther. That was my misconception. Almost effortlessly, the nimble creatures bound up and over the rock face.

I quickly rummaged through my pack, looking frantically for my camera, but succeeded in capturing only a single photo before the entire group of bighorns disappeared over the summit. As the sun began to fade prematurely behind the towering walls, the colors of the reddish sandstone took on a gentler pinkish hue. Soon, another previously hidden canyon came into view.

This would make an ideal campsite, I thought. So following the ravine several hundred feet, I eventually came upon a stone stairway. The unique formation had been created by both wind and water, and at its base was a cold, clear spring. The water emerged from somewhere deep within the earth. I began to set up my crude campground and decided to give the location a special name. In the light, the rocks formed a staircase of sorts and the circular formation circled skyward; hence, the name should reflect its apparent destination. So as the final rays of light faded to black, I looked up at the twinkling stars shining down on one of the most peaceful places on earth. I convinced myself I had just discovered the stairway to heaven.

By first light, I was anxious to discover what hidden treasures I might find by climbing up the narrow canyon. Countless flash floods cascading off the plateau above me had scooped out pockets in the soft sandstone. Carefully I grasped the small handholds in the rock wall and began to climb upward. This undiscovered arroyo was no place to break a leg or, worse yet, my neck. But still, this entire journey was all about adventure; and by its very definition, adventure was any journey that contained a certain element of risk. So step by careful step, I climbed higher and higher into the unknown.

At one point, I realized it was possible. If I continued to climb any higher, I might not be able to get back down. It looked as though I may be near the top, so whispering a silent prayer, I squeezed my body up between the narrow chasm and pulled myself up and over the final hurdle. What I discovered was a solid lock ledge twenty or thirty feet wide. It was as if I had scrambled my way to the top of the world with a vast expanse of desert below me. The hidden valley, the slow meandering river with buttes and red rock spires spread before me, as far as the eye could see.

No words could describe the beauty. And the emotions, which welled up inside me, were also beyond description. Truly, I had climbed the stairway to heaven; and as I sat there watching the sun rise into a perfect cloudless sky, I made one final discovery. The purpose for my arduous journey into the magical hidden valley and the discovery of the weathered stone staircase led me to the missing key to Camelot.

I was, it turned out, not the first of my kind to arrive here. Faded images scratched deeply into the manganese coating almost chest high on the cliff face told the tale. A series of petroglyphs depicted a small band of ancient hunters who had pursued the desert bighorns into their once-safe haven. The evidence of what was apparently a successful hunt was also portrayed on the panel.

The large fully curled horns of the slain animal left little doubt the herd leader, a mighty ram, had perished that day. Other sheep were also depicted fleeing from the hunters. Ewes and lambs and what may have been younger males were etched into the sandstone wall. But lower and slightly to the left was another drawing. This depiction was partially hidden behind the leafy branches of a single-leaf ash. The crude etching depicted three stick figures.

Possibly drawn by children who were following the hunting party, these depictions were of a different creature: an animal that had evolved in North America millions of years before the arrival of mankind. These animals would leave behind their fossilized remains in the tar pits of California buried beneath the sandy dunes of southern Utah. They possessed a unique characteristic unlike any other ungulate on the planet, which allowed them to survive in the harshest, most inhospitable places on earth.

The distinct hump on their back stored fat, which could be used to sustain these hardy creatures when the bitter cold or scorching heat shriveled their food resources. Mine would be the only remote desert lodge in all of North America that offered its guests a trek into the rugged backcountry riding an animal, which was far better suited than the common horse. A creature superbly designed to travel across this arid land. And only one small addition would be required to change my new lodge's chosen name.

Camelot, from now on, would be divided into two words as opposed to one. And to make better sense, a *the* would be added at the beginning to tie it all together. From point forward, I would call my future home after an animal it would honor. The Camel-Lot would bring happiness and adventure to hundreds of visitors. Far into the distance, I could barely make out the outline of a small town nestled at the base of the La Sal Mountain Range.

To the north was the world-famous Arches National Park. And to the south and west were the vast and scenic Canyonlands. Hopefully somewhere in between luck and perseverance, I would find my perfect home.

Camping on Kane Creek Road

ONCE I RETURNED to camp, I busied myself by eliminating all traces of my stay. The makeshift bed I had constructed of pine boughs was scattered beneath the trees, and the small campfire was buried and swept clean with a sagebrush broom. It was highly unlikely that anyone would discover the canyon or, for that matter, follow my footprints into the hidden valley; but just in case, I would leave it as pristine as I found it. I wanted to keep this location a secret for long.

Steven shared my love of the great outdoors, so when he came to visit, I would bring him here. I was hopeful that someday I would meet the woman whom I would spend the rest of my life with and she too would share in the magic of my discoveries. But for now, only Jinda, once she arrived from Alaska, would be with me to further explore this place.

I arrived in Moab by early afternoon. Typical of many small Mormon towns scattered throughout the state, a church and a large city park for activities after church were the primary structures. The homes and yards, for the most part, were neat and tidy; but something about this place was very atypical.

First settled by the Ute Indians, the Mormon settlers were driven out of Moab shortly after their arrival. Rumor has it one of the chief's daughters was offered as a bride to a church elder in a gesture of friendship. Considered to be a heathen, the gift was rejected. This would lead to bad blood between the two parties. The once-hospitable Ute tribe showed the arrogant impostors the door, and until the discovery of uranium in 1933, few whites dared show their face here. One exception was an occasional miner or explorer.

Currently, Moab was considered to be the adventure capital of the state, and anything and everything pertaining to the outdoors was big business here. Mountain biking and river rafting seemed to be the major draw. At times, there were as many bicycles on the roadways as there were cars. Mega trucks dragging long trailers were loaded with colorful rafts and made their way along the winding River Road. These caravans would take visitors from far and wide to drop-off points along the mighty Colorado.

Single-day excursions offered adventure seekers an opportunity to challenge the rapids locally. Those with sufficient time and money could opt for a multiday trip through class 4 and 5 rapids in the legendary Cataract Canyon. Class 4 equates to multiple opportunities to examine the bottom of the river while hanging on upside down in an inverted raft. Class 5 rapids entail drafting your last will and testament prior to departure, then dropping over twenty-foot falls in a raging river to the jagged rocks below, all the while praying to multiple gods just in case yours isn't listening. All kidding aside, Colorado River guides are some of the most experienced and knowledgeable in the world; and on the two occasions, I had the chance to raft down the river with them. I was privileged to have them taking such great care of me.

I pulled into the parking lot of the only major grocery store in town. The thought of eating something that wasn't plucked from a bush or dug up out of the ground sounded very appealing just now. I suppose I looked a little ragged, but then so did 90 percent of my fellow shoppers. Hikers, bikers, river rafters, and rock climbers wandered the isles, loading up on trail mix and cheap beer.

Everyone knows shopping when you're starving is not a good idea, so with what started out to be bagels and a jar of peanut butter, that adventure turned into a grocery cart full of everything I shouldn't eat with a bag of apples to convince myself I was really eating healthy. When I returned to the parking lot, stuffing my face with pastries and cold milk, I noticed a small building at the far end of the street. The structure was fairly nondescript. Built mostly of brick, measuring perhaps a thousand square feet in size, it did have one very noticeable attraction. A four-by-eight weathered sign was secured with rusted lag bolts to a metal pole in the small front yard. The lettering appeared to have been stenciled by hand, but the words Real Estate for Sale got my blood pumping.

I considered checking into a campground and taking a shower, but barged in the door of a real estate office anyway. How would these strangers react to my far-fetched dreams of a wilderness lodge that offered exotic camel treks? I hadn't shaved in a week, and I looked more like a homeless vagrant than an entrepreneur. But this wasn't the Ritz-Carlton, so I changed into my last somewhat-clean wool shirt and headed toward the office. I hoped it wouldn't turn out to be another fruitless search for land for sale.

The rustic wooden door needed a new paint job, and the hinges needed oil; but when I peered inside, everything was clean and appeared orderly. A gal was sitting behind a large metal desk and looked up with a genuine smile.

"Hi," she said. "Come in and close the door. How can I help you?"

The shower idea would have been a good one, I thought as I extended my hand and introduced myself.

"I'm looking for land. A remote location, if possible, as far from town as you've got." Damn, I sounded like a bank robber hiding from the law. "I would like to build a guest lodge here where I have plans to offer camel rides."

Her eyebrows rose up ever so slightly. "Really! Camels? That's something we don't have here yet."

I was beginning to feel a little foolish. Maybe I should keep the whole camel idea to myself. I'd only arrived in town less than an hour ago, and already I was certain the only person I had spoken with thought I was a raving lunatic. Before I continued my ramblings, an office door on my left swung open; and a man, approximately my own height and weight, strode into the room. He was dressed in casual attire, jeans, boots, and a dark T-shirt tucked neatly into his pants. His hair was cut short, and he had the look of a man who spent time in the outdoors.

"Randy Day," he said, grasping my hand firmly. He had a broad smile, and there was a small gap between his front teeth. In spite of his somewhat-used-car salesman approach, he looked like someone you could trust. His next statement, however, almost sent me reeling.

"So you're looking for someplace remote, huh? I think I might have just what you want."

Well, that was easy. Months of searching, talking to every real estate agent from Cedar City to Blanding, and a man I met less than thirty seconds ago has just what I'm looking for.

"I have an appointment now I'm already late for," he said. "Meet me here at 8 a.m. tomorrow, and we'll run out and take a look at it."

Before I could inquire as to the price of the land he spoke of or its general direction, he was out the door and gone. I turned back to Gail as if to say, "Who the hell was that" as she handed me a business card and, still smiling, opened the door to let me out. I'm not exactly sure how long I wandered around the small town of Moab, but for whatever reason, it already felt like home.

I stopped by a small roadside café that catered mostly to the locals. There were really only three or four items on the menu: burritos, tacos, and drinks. I looked around and discovered the burritos were about the same dimensions as a size 12 tennis shoe. It was filled with everything from meat to rice to beans and homemade salsa. They smelled great, so I ordered two. One for now and one to go. I asked the waitress about a good place to camp, and she directed me to a little canyon a mile or so south of town.

"There is a little spring on the left side of the road past some cottonwoods," she said. "It's pretty quiet out there, and the water's good to drink."

Thanking her for the tip, I filled up my soda from the machine and headed south.

Kane Creek Road would be a place I would get to know intimately over the next few years. Not only was it a great place to camp, it would also be the road that would finally take me home.

The Road to Camelot

I 'VE NEVER CONSIDERED myself a particularly religious person, but there was a man who was very influential to me in my youth. He told me there are angels on earth who watch over people.

"If your heart is true and your spirit is clean, these invisible angles will speak to you," he said. "And they will help direct you in life."

Samuel Bagay was not a man of wealth or someone with political influence. He was in fact a simple shepherd. Born and raised on a Navajo Indian Reservation, Samuel grew up in a world without even the simple, basic necessities. Running water, electricity, or even shoes were not a part of his early childhood.

I had been sent to live on a boys' ranch in southern Utah, and they told us about an Indian who grazed sheep in the forest a half mile or so from the property. We were instructed to stay away from his trailer and not to disturb him. But this was a full-blooded Navajo, I told my inquisitive self. He might possess the legendary knowledge of all living things. This man could be a mentor, I thought. If I could just sit in his presence, the secrets he kept of the universe might somehow seep into my body; or at least, that is what my young, idealistic mind convinced me.

Raised by his grandmother, Samuel had few memories of his father and mother. Both died in a car accident on the way home from a rodeo in New Mexico. The drunk driver survived the crash, but left a small boy – only seven years old – an orphan and a Navajo village devastated.

Samuel told me there are no orphans among his people; so rather than be shipped off to live in foster homes, he was blessed as I was to have a new loving, caring, and very strict (*shima*) mother.

When I approached the open trailer door, my heart was in my throat. I had no idea how I would explain the intrusion. Perhaps I could say I was lost or orphaned. Maybe he would take me in and raise me as his own. As you can tell, I watched Billy Jack movies one too many times. Do I knock? Sit outside the door and wait? I pondered the questions briefly, but then a powerful-looking gray-and-white Australian sheepdog solved the dilemma for me. Appearing in the doorway was the no-named canine. He let out a bark and, jumping from the stoop, approached me cautiously. I let him sniff my hand but didn't try petting the dog. I knew from experience some animals didn't like being cuddled. This wasn't a pet, it was a working sheepdog, and playing fetch or heeling on a leash was probably not part of his daily routine.

"Well, my dog likes you," the voice from the shadows said. He stepped from the trailer into the bright sunlight.

"How can you tell?" I asked.

"He didn't eat you," he answered.

I looked at the narrow weathered brown face and the deep-set dark brown eyes. I imagined he would have long dark hair worn in a braid. I probably assumed he would also have eagle feathers in his headband. Aren't Indians supposed to be clad from head to toe in deerskin breeches and a fringed leather shirt? Fooled again by my imagination. His hair was in fact cut short, slightly gray around the edges, but full and neat. His Levi's jeans were well worn and matched the rest of his cowboy-looking attire including a light blue checkered country shirt and pointed-toe cowboy boots.

I wasn't invited inside. In fact, during the entire two years I visited Samuel Bagay at his trailer, I never once viewed its interior. He pointed, Navajo-style, with his pursed lips at a foldout wooden chair by a still-smoldering campfire. I sat down and thought for a moment I should explain the reason for my visit. But when I looked back at his smiling, relaxed face, I realized there was a welcoming wisdom in those eyes beyond his forty-seven years.

He knew why I had come. We were both running from the demons that haunted us. Both looking for same answers to the age-old question, "Why me?"

During my many visits to Samuel Bagay's camp, I learned of his difficult, poverty-stricken childhood. His stories never really gave any indication he was looking for sympathy. They were simply matter-of-fact.

"Water on the reservation," he explained, "was shipped in by tanker."

The small earthen one-room hogan was his home. Meals, consisting mostly of mutton and corn bread, were usually prepared in his grandmother's single earthly possession, a steel pot. She had a small flock of sheep that provided both meat and wool. The wool was hand-spun into yarn, which could be woven into blankets or sold to buy corn, the other staple food in his diet. Cash from the sale of yarn would also purchase the few other items necessary to survive.

Eventually, Samuel was rounded up with the other Indian children and forced to move to a missionary-run school where he was disciplined harshly for almost everything he did, including speaking Navajo – the only language he had ever known.

Bitterness led to anger. Anger eventually led to alcohol. The journey that brought him here to a small trailer in the forest was a pursuit to reconnect with the only happiness he had ever known. A simple existence surrounded by the animals he loved, far away from a troubled past and the drinking that led to a failed marriage, expulsion from his tribe, and so much despair.

One evening while sitting by the fire outside the small silver trailer, he asked me if I knew the importance of a pact. Of course, I had a vague understanding that a pact referred to an agreement between two parties to live up to a promise. I asked him to explain his question in more detail, so he went on to reveal the strong temptation he had struggled with to stay away from the bottle. To avoid becoming like my own father, I had never tried so much as a beer.

We would, he decided, form a pact sealed in fire. He agreed to never again put a bottle to his lips. And for my part, I would promise to never take a drink.

In the summer of '69, Samuel Bagay moved to Arizona to live with a cousin. I visited him on only two other occasions. He attended my high school graduation, and I saw him after returning from my four-year stint in the U.S. Navy. At the time I made the agreement, I had no idea what life-altering ramifications our solemn oath we made to each other would have.

My friend would depart this earth twenty-two years later from kidney failure. But keeping his promise, Samuel Bagay never took another drink of alcohol. And although severely tempted on many occasions, I kept my end of the bargain as well.

On my recent fifty-fifth birthday, I toasted the celebration with friends and family with seven glasses of champagne and a single glass of apple juice. My angel had indeed watched over me.

*   *   *

Try as I might, sleep would not come easily that night. At 3:00 a.m., I dozed off at last. In five more hours, Randy Day would take me to the place I had been diligently searching for. I hoped the three long months I spent painting this picture in my head of a perfect desert paradise would be discovered at last. As truly remarkable as my journey had been, I was ready to settle down and begin the task of building my home.

I arrived thirty minutes early, so I ducked into City Market for doughnuts and milk. I wasn't sure if Randy liked pastries for breakfast, but I hoped the bribe would bring us luck on our trip. In addition to the sweets, I stocked up on Spam and potatoes for an evening meal. He arrived late, so I paced anxiously back and forth for fifteen long minutes. I briefly considered starting his porch on fire for making me wait but opted instead to eat his doughnuts.

When he showed up in the big sparkling new white Chevy pickup, he was smiling from ear to ear. Immediately all my anxieties disappeared. Swinging the passenger door open, he slid his leather briefcase over.

"Buckle up," he said. "We'll be going down a bumpy road, and I don't wanna lose ya."

We headed in the direction that, only a few minutes earlier, I had come from. When we turned onto Kane Springs Road, I had to laugh.

"This is it?" I asked.

"We aren't there yet," he replied.

The eighteen miles of rugged dirt road would take more than an hour to traverse, even at these breakneck speeds. As we drove, Randy told me a little bit about his life here. A Moab native, Randy worked in the uranium mines in the early '70s. Driving five-ton ore trucks in and out of canyons like this was a hard life. The job paid well, he said, but the radioactive dust he inhaled led to a fight with cancer that nearly cost him his life.

Married, Randy had five children ages six to sixteen and began a career in real estate three years ago. Currently, the real estate business was booming.

"The once-quiet little mining town had at last been discovered. Two national parks and three state parks are right out our back doors. The Colorado River flowed by at the edge of town and homes that only a few years earlier were sold for thirty thousand dollars, but now are sold for four times that amount."

The exhilaration I felt an hour earlier was replaced with hopeless desperation.

"We should probably head back to town," I said. "This is probably a waste of time."

"Why is that?" he asked.

"I don't have that kind of money," I mumbled. "My meager savings of fifty-three thousand dollars seemed like a vast fortune this morning, but probably wouldn't even pay for the property taxes."

"We're almost there," he said, coming to a halt at the top of a large plateau.

Exiting the truck, I followed him to the edge of an overlook. On the metal pole cemented into the ground held a sign: Hurrah Pass Elevation 5,000 Feet. It turned out that an old cattle rancher by the name of Jackson once ran cattle in this rugged canyon. There was no road at that time, so the only way to get the cows to market involved bringing the herd single file, up and over what was once a very narrow sheep trail. A good year meant all cattle and cowboys made it out alive. After counting heads, the men would take off their hats and holler, you guessed it, hurrah!

The road continued several more miles into the endless abyss below. We stood, silently gazing down upon everything I had dreamed of and maybe more. Every color of red you could imagine was painted on the towering spires, which jutted a thousand feet into the bright blue sky. Coyote willows and green leaves of the Fremont cottonwood trees lined the muddy riverbank while blue sage and towering yucca dotted the valley floor.

Looking down on the future home of Camelot Lodge from Hurrah Pass

Far off the distance, Saddle Horn Butte and Dead Horse Point State Park stood etched into the steep cliffs. This vast expanse of the multimillion-acre Canyonlands National Park encircled the valley below. Every view in every direction was breathtaking. The mighty Colorado River had carved this region since the dawn of time and still flowed peacefully only a couple of miles away.

The longer I stood there, the more I realized the price tag for any property this stunning was way out of my league.

"What do you think?" Randy said, breaking me out of my morose stupor.

"Is this it?" I asked.

"No, it's down there."

I followed his finger pointing toward a small island in the middle of the river.

"Forty-eight point eight acres, right on the banks of the river."

"Randy, I am really sorry," I said. "I can't afford an acre of land on the river not to mention fifty."

"How do you know? I haven't even told you the price."

"Well, are you going to tell me or do we just stand here dreaming some more?"

"Fifty-two thousand dollars," he announced. That was about one-fiftieth of the amount of money I had. This was worse than I thought. What was I thinking?

Fifty-two thousand dollars an acre was certainly reasonable for such a beautiful property, but my mind went to numb when trying to calculate the total cost. Why bother.

"Want to drive down and take a look?" Randy said.

"Look, I only have around fifty-three thousand dollars, Randy. With no job and no credit, the future wasn't looking so bright anymore."

"So you'll have a thousand dollars left over. And that's the best deal you'll find around here."

"What's the total cost of the property?" I was a little confused here.

"I told you. Fifty-two thousand dollars!"

"Please don't BS me. I've been traveling for a long time, looking for a place to build a ranch. I never dreamed it would be this beautiful, so if this is some kind of joke, tell me now."

"Should we go down and have a closer look at your new camel ranch? Or do you want to go on dreaming about it?"

As the last of the hooting and hollering echoed off the canyon walls, we jumped into the truck to complete the final leg of the journey to the most beautiful ranch in all of Utah. As we drove down the narrow twisting, winding dirt road, I once more began to daydream. In my mind, I imagined the lodge with a huge picture window looking out the winding, tranquil river. On a narrow bluff, there would be a large fenced pasture and a barn. I could see a hitching post with a saddle draped over it. Grazing in the pasture, two elegant camels gracefully raised their long necks to look far into the distance.

Although we had not yet arrived, within minutes, I would be setting foot on the land that had been calling to me since I dreamed of its existence a lifetime ago on a frozen lake in Alaska. We were rounding the bend in the road when a survey marker next to a real estate sign came into view.

"This is it," Randy said. I jumped out of the truck and walked over to the sign that read, Land for Sale. I yanked it from the ground and tossed it into the truck.

"Not anymore," I said. "This land is sold." With tears of joy welling up in my eyes, I scooped up a handful of the soft red sand and let it trickle through my fingers. One long adventure was over, and another was about to begin.

"Welcome to the Camel-Lot," I said. Randy, who was still smiling in the front seat of the truck, replied.

"Write me a check, and it's a done deal."

I would be almost broke, but there was no doubt this was everything I had hoped for and more. My hands were shaking.

"This is one of the happiest days of my life."

Following My Heart

A S I WANDERED through the small canyon dividing the property, I came upon a wide circular bowl. Two rocks stood poised, balancing on the skyline like sentries guarding the hidden treasures of this mystical place. The giant boulders were strewn about like an unfinished marble game left behind by mythological gods. I knelt down and ran my palm over the smooth Cutler sandstone. Warn and weathered for millions of years, this was a colorful ancient stone-sculpted masterpiece. Various shades of red and pink were interspersed with hues of deep purple blended haphazardly in the rolling petrified dunes.

Saddle Horn Butte

The vertical walls appeared to have been sifted into layers. Like a fine dessert, the slabs of stone looked as though they were sliced while still frozen, then drizzled with dark chocolate. Oceans and rivers had, at one time, flooded this entire region; so small fossils embedded in small pockets of baked mud revealed evidence of a changed world.

Randy pointed out a series of egg-sized footprints leading away from what may have been a pool. Partially buried in drifting sand, whatever animal left these tracks behind vanished with a host of other creatures long before mankind's arrival. Dinosaur tracks like these made the Canyonlands a magnet for geologists, paleontologists, and rock hounds from around the country.

"Hard to imagine there were creatures like mastodons, saber-toothed cats, and giant sloths once living here," Randy said.

"And camels," I added.

"Really? I thought camels were from the Middle East."

"Most people think that. But the first fossils ever found were actually discovered somewhere in Nebraska or the Dakotas," I shared.

"Well, who'da thought."

When we reached the summit, the river came into view a short distance ahead. I realized my little piece of heaven was only a stone's throw away from the water. But where exactly was the property line?

"How far is my place from the river?" I asked.

"All the way to the edge," he answered.

As much as I really didn't want to know the answer, I had to ask, "How is it possible, Randy, that forty-eight acres of riverfront property only costs around twelve hundred dollars an acre?"

"The road scares the hell out of most people," he said. "And building a house all the way out here will take ten times as long as it would in town. There are no power lines, so you'll need a generator or maybe solar panels. They haven't had much luck drilling a well with drinkable water, and everything from flash floods to rattlesnakes will probably scare off any future wife. Sure this is what you want?"

This guy had no idea where I had just moved from. As we made our way down toward the river, whiptail lizards darted through the yellow blossoms of the mule's ears, and antelope and ground squirrels ducked into their burrows beneath the Mormon tea. Tracks of coyote, kit fox, and mule deer were scattered along a sandy wash. Everywhere I looked, there were signs of life. A great blue heron sounded an alarm cry and flapped its giant wings as it rose into the sky and soared downstream in search of a quieter fishing hole.

As we waded out into the shallow, muddy water, I told Randy a little bit about my previous home in the Alaska wilderness.

"This place," I said, "is a walk in the park. Besides, I love rattlesnake, and any woman crazy enough to hook up with me will probably be crazy enough to love them too."

I really never fully understood how a person could fall so deeply in love with a piece of ground, but as we walked the entire perimeter of the property, I began to feel that love.

No human, I told myself, could be better suited for this little piece of heaven. Tomorrow I would trade in my little car for a truck capable of navigating the rugged road, but for tonight, I would pitch my tent on the banks of the peaceful river. There were papers to sign back in Randy's office, but they just have wait.

The only way I could convince myself this place was really mine was to spread my blanket on the ground and look up into the night sky and declare it to be just so. Randy shook my hand, and with my entire life savings in his capable hands, he headed back to town to get the paperwork started.

"This is my place now, right?" I asked as he began to drive away.

"All yours," he said, hanging his head out the window. "I'll bring a boat down in the morning to pick you up."

"I won't be hard to find."

Twenty minutes later, I watched the white Chevy pickup disappear over Hurrah Pass. It was a long, exciting journey, but I was happy to finally be home. Steven, my nephew in Salt Lake, said "I told you so" when I called to tell him about my new home in Moab. But I wouldn't have missed the journey getting here for anything in the world.

Dueling with the Daltons

BY MORNING, ANY lingering doubts regarding my hasty decision had vanished. My first night camping by the river reassured me that I would be living in paradise. Just before dawn, a doe and her fawn came warily to the river's edge to drink. A beaver dragging fresh-cut willows to a small island in the center of the river caught the protective mother deer's attention. Her large ears rotated forward, but sensing no danger, she lowered her muzzle into the murky water.

Far off in the distance, a family of coyotes began to yip and howl a greeting to a new day. Slowly I turned my head in the direction of the chorus and then looked back in the direction of the deer, but they had quietly disappeared back into the thicket.

Watching the morning sunrise over Hurrah Pass, I listened to all the sounds of nature begin to change shifts. Creatures of the night, including small brown bats diving erratically over the water for a final feast of moths and gnats, suddenly abandoned their hunt and sought out a deep crevasse in the fractured Cutler sandstone cliffs. They would remain in their roost till dusk, and the insectivorous cliff swallows would take over the task of devouring the multitude of pesky bugs that never seemed to diminish.

Spadefoot toads burrowed beneath the roots of the Fremont cottonwood trees while bullfrogs lie in wait in the shadows of the tamarisk for a passing cricket or darkling beetle. A Canadian goose and her goslings swam out of the willows, and turkey vultures soared on the early-morning thermals, gliding effortlessly over Saddle Horn Butte.

I climbed up on the small ridge dividing the property, and as the warming rays of the sun reflected off the towering cliffs, I sat in awe. The sights, the sounds, the sweet smells of evening primrose and sand verbena all painted a lovelier picture than I could have ever imagined.

Somewhere in my pack was breakfast. The slightly bruised apple and crushed granola bar would have to suffice until my ride showed up. I would treat myself to a celebratory breakfast when I returned to Moab to sign the documents finalizing the deal. For now, however, anything to quiet the rumbling in my stomach would be a feast. I remained up on the small ridge, admiring the view until the sound of horse hooves clambering over the rocks snapped me out of my daze.

A few moments later, I saw two riders pushing a small group of cattle over the dunes. One of the riders appeared to be a child, a young girl perhaps ten or twelve years old. The second rider was an elderly gentleman. Even from a distance, it was obvious this man had spent a great deal of time in a saddle. There was a graceful flowing motion between the horse and the elderly rider, and the small child had been well tutored in the art of equine management.

I scrambled out of the rocks to meet my new neighbors, but my friendly greeting was not returned in a similar fashion. Val Dalton was a third-generation cattle rancher, and the valley I was squatting on belonged, in his mind, to him and his cows.

"I'm your new neighbor," I said, extending my hand.

"I've only got two neighbors, and you ain't one of 'em."

"I just bought this property, and I intend to build my home here."

I was hoping to keep the conversation friendly, but Mr. Dalton wasn't exactly making it easy. I looked up at his weathered brown face. The worn straw cowboy hat on his head was soiled in sweat, and the once-white flannel shirt was a faded dusty gray. Fences were going up all over the west, and the once-open range was quickly becoming a cluster of small ratchets. Old ranching families like the Daltons were getting squeezed out, and although he knew in his heart the results were inevitable, he wasn't going down without a fight.

"Sir, I'm not looking for a fight here. You're welcome to graze your cattle on my land if you'll keep them out of my garden."

The young girl looked down and smiled. "Grandpa's a little grumpy in the morning," she said as her dishwater blond hair draped down over her lean tan face.

"That's okay," I said. "I get that way myself sometimes."

Val gave the palomino a gentle nudge and looked back with a final warning.

"You can't close down a cattle trail to the river," he said

"I bought your cow trail, Mr. Dalton, but we'll leave the trail open just the same for now."

The girl sauntered her pony alongside the old man. His shoulders seemed to sag. The life of a cowboy had always been incredibly difficult. Working from dusk till dawn, success or failure depended on countless challenges with many of them not within your control. I watched the proud old man and his granddaughter disappear over the ridge. It might take some time, I thought, but Val Dalton and I would be friends someday. It would be many months later and in the wake of disaster that we met again. The next time, he would know me as a friend.

*   *   *

I looked up at the sound of a truck coming over the top of Hurrah Pass. The white Chevy was leaving a trail of dust as it made its rapid descent. I guess my first boat ride up the Colorado River wouldn't be happening today. I packed my bag and settled down on the shade of a large boulder. Most drivers would need a half hour or more to make it down the winding, bumpy dirt road. Randy would make it in half the time.

By the time I got to the junction of the wash that would serve as my driveway, he was just rounding the final bend. The big friendly smile was a welcome relief after my run-in with Val. I jumped in the front seat and returned the offered handshake.

"How was your first night?" he said.

"Everything I knew it would be," I answered.

"Want your money back?"

"You gotta be kidding."

The delicious smell of sausage filled the cab of the truck.

"Thought you might like some breakfast," he said, passing me a white McDonald's bag.

I never knew how good a McMuffin could taste till I opened the wrapper and devoured the sandwich in two bites, then washing it down with the small carton of orange juice. I looked up slightly embarrassed at having eaten his doughnuts the previous morning.

"Thanks," I said. "It sure beats a cold can of Spam."

"Ready to head back to town?" he asked.

"Not really," I said. "I better find a truck that can get me out here, or I'll be swimming the river to get home."

He turned the truck around in the tight wash and began to head back up the boulder-strewn road.

"I know you don't have a lot of money left," Randy said. "So I made a couple of phone calls and found you a job. I hope you don't mind."

This was unbelievable. Not only did this man take me to the most perfect property I could imagine then offered it at a price I could afford, but also now he brought me breakfast and found me a job. This guy was my hero! If I was ever inclined to hug another man, now would be the time; but with a five-hundred-foot drop-off only ten feet or so past the driver's side door, I opted instead for a sincere thanks and a slap on the back.

*   *   *

Paul Cox was a local contractor in town and also served on the bench as the elected judge. Paul and Randy were longtime friends. Since it had been a few years since I had pounded nails, this job was a great opportunity to refresh my building skills. Besides, my dwindling bank account was beginning to weigh heavily on me.

If I worked for Paul five days a week on a paying job, I could spend the weekends at Camelot building my lodge. It would probably take more than a year to get up and running, but the hardest part of the job – finding the perfect location – was done.

With my optimistic enthusiasm, I assumed building a three-thousand-foot guest lodge in the middle of nowhere would be easy, but the next three exhausting years would teach me different. It would entail more physically demanding labor and mentally challenging responsibility than I could ever have previously endured. But on that glorious spring day, I headed into Moab with a song in my heart and a bright new future looming ahead. Everything and anything was possible; and today, I thought, was the first day of a very grand adventure.

The Princess of Camelot

Month old terror Lady Gwennivere

S INCE I FINALLY had a place to call home, it was time to send for my dog, Jinda. I dearly missed her but wasn't exactly sure how the resilient little bear dog from the north would do in this new land. My life and the many new adventures I would experience here would certainly not be complete without her.

As it turned out, Jinda's foster mom, Marcee, was driving south from Anchorage to visit her family in Oregon. She offered to drive Jinda the extra distance to Salt Lake to meet me. Everything was at last falling into place, but I needed to take some time to gather my thoughts. I decided to spend a few days with my favorite nephew, Steven, and his wife. The timing was perfect as they were expecting their first child. When I exited the car, I could see excitement in his face. Becoming a new father was the only thing missing in this fine man's life.

The ultrasound indicated the pregnancy was going well and the new baby would be a girl. Life was about to take a radical turn for Steve and Ruth, and I would become a proud great-uncle. I didn't realize how much I missed my canine companion, and I couldn't wait to see her. I received the call early Saturday morning. Marcee and Jinda had been driving most of the night, but they had just crossed into Utah and would be arriving in a few hours.

I paced like an expectant father in the maternity ward. Steven had never met Jinda, but he had certainly heard every story ever told about the wonderful little dog. He excitedly anticipated their first meeting. I expressed to him my concerns about all the new dangers Jinda would face in her new home. There were prickly spines on the cactus, stings from the giant hairy scorpions, and the dreaded bite from the faded midget rattlesnake that could seriously injure or kill a small dog. Steve dismissed my concerns with a straightforward logical statement.

"For the last several years, she's lived with thousand-pound grizzlies and run with wolf packs that would have devoured most dogs. I think she'll figure it all out," he said calmly.

He was right; Jinda would survive the desert in the same way she survived in Alaska. Her superb cunning and skill combined with an overprotective father would protect her from almost anything. The moment she jumped from the car was as if she had never left. Ruth wasn't really a dog person, but within a few moments, Jinda charmed everyone. Including Ruth. If I ever had to leave town, it was nice to know that Jinda could stay with them. Steven instantly bonded with my polite little dog, and I hoped they'd remain friends throughout her lifetime. The following morning, we headed south to Moab. It would be Jinda's final home.

On my first day of construction, I realized how much I had forgotten about building with a hammer and nails. While training animals in the 1980s, there were always the slow times due to writers' strikes, union disagreements, or other production shutdowns. There was also a host of movies that just didn't need animals. During those times, I would hire local contractors as framers. I had no idea at the time how crucial the trade would be in my future.

With lots of time but a lack of money, I decided my work with Paul could be mutually beneficial. If I could pick his brain on everything and anything I might need to know in building my own house, it's possible I could actually pull this off for a fraction of the cost. He graciously agreed to order all my building materials on his account at the local hardware store. With a 20–30 percent reduction in the cost of materials, I hoped to build the lodge for about a hundred and fifty thousand. That was a hundred and forty-nine thousand more than I had.

But when in doubt, borrow.

With that in mind, I began contacting every lending institution I could find. Most advertised you would receive an answer in fifteen minutes or less, and with that usually being the case, the answer was always the same. No!

After a hard, backbreaking day at work, I would often drive down a paved road located on the opposite side of the river. To do this carefully, I would have to navigate my boat along the swift current of the river. The pavement ended in plain view of my newly purchased property, and cars don't float. The road was indeed a blessing, but looking down on the place I longed to be was not the same as being there.

On moonlit nights, Jinda and I would sit outside my tent and gaze down on our future home. Close, but just out of reach. On one hand, the peaceful flowing river was an unexpected bonus; but on the other hand, it was also a deterrent in my getting home. I wondered why such a nice dead-end road was built in the middle of nowhere. I found brochure in the visitors' center in town that answered the question for me. While drilling for oil back in the sixties, a deep pocket of potash was discovered along the river corridor. Used in everything from road salt to fertilizer, the decision was made to build a processing plant at the site. Large evaporation ponds were constructed to dry the deposits once they were pumped to the surface. To access the new development, they needed a road.

The giant blue drying beds were a terrible eyesore, but the good-paying jobs brought to Moab and surrounding towns were a blessing. Being so close to Canyonlands National Park was a major concern to the environmental groups, but little heed was paid to their protests. Then like now, the almighty dollar made potential environmental disasters fade to black. Until a more suitable mode of transportation could be located, the paved road on the wrong side of the Colorado River would have to suffice. It was about all the little Honda could handle.

There was a small pullout on the top of a ridge, and abandoned fire pits suggested it had been used as a temporary campground. For the time being, it would have to suffice as my home. A well-worn trail down the river provided access to water, and we would be able to bathe and fish. Jinda loved to swim in the shallow water and became obsessed with a family of beavers, which cruised back and forth across the river carrying ample-cut willows to their lodge on the opposite side. There I could see the small sandbar where I had spent my first night on the property. Tomorrow morning, I had one crucial task: find a boat.

Randy stopped by the job site a few days later with some good news. An old schoolmate of his worked at a local car dealership, and he informed Randy about a used truck he had for sale. He thought the pickup was in good-enough shape to make it over the pass and had agreed to take my car in trade. That is, if I was interested. We met with the car salesman, Mike, that evening. He was about the best used-car dealer in the county, but I wasn't buying his sales pitch just yet. We went to the very back of the lot. That's where they kept the vehicles that were one step above a recycled Pepsi can. The old black Ford wasn't the prettiest truck I had ever seen, but it appeared to be mechanically sound. Best of all, its four-wheel drive was capable of getting me on the right side of the river. I was elated but wondered if Mike would sweeten the deal a little.

"What did you have in mind?" he asked.

On the other side of a chain-link fence, outside the body shop, was an old aluminum Grumman canoe. It looked a little beat-up, but as far as I could tell, it would float.

"Throw in the canoe and we have a deal," I said.

Mike scratched his head for a moment as if he was working on a counteroffer when Randy chimed in.

"Give him the dang canoe. You haven't had that thing in the water since we were in high school," he said.

"He might agree to take you on a camel ride someday." Mike laughed at the idea of riding on a camel but handed me the keys to the truck.

"Take it over the pass," he said. "If you like it, it's yours. I'll see if I can find the paddles that go with the canoe."

Before heading home, I stopped by the grocery store for a steak and baking potatoes. I would also need some dog treats for Jinda and a sparkling bottle of apple cider.

"Time to celebrate!" I said. "The truck may look like an old beater to the rest of the world, but to me, it was a chariot."

June 2, 1998: Today was my sister Jody's fortieth birthday. It was also the day I broke ground on Camelot Adventure Lodge. With little more than a pick and shovel, I began digging the footings for my new home. Every cinder block, every bag of concrete, every two-by-four, and nail would come over the tortuous gravel road – one truckload at a time. The cement would then have to be shoveled into a generator-powered mixer. I had absolutely no idea how long my half-ton Ford truck would hold up, but one thing was for sure, I was building my lodge even if I had to deliver the whole thing in the bottom of an eighteen-foot canoe.

Little by little, the lodge began to take shape. By the time fall arrived, the three-fourth-inch plywood deck was complete. I could now sleep under the stars in my make-believe living room on my make-believe couch. Jinda spent most days exploring every nook and cranny on the property. The bears of Redoubt Bay had been replaced by pesky cows. At long last, the little cattle dog from Alaska could practice the skills she was born with: putting cows in their place. The cows, she decided, could graze anywhere they pleased. Anywhere that is, except the forty-eight acres of land belonging to her.

With winter right around the corner, my plans to have a roof over my head by first snowfall were looking next to impossible. Even by working seven days a week, twelve to fourteen hours a day, there was no way I could meet my intended deadline. The Amasa Back Loop located five miles past the property was one of the most grueling bike trails in the country. Mountain bikers from Germany, Japan, France, and every corner of the United States traveled to the little town of Moab to attempt the harrowing ride.

The first few miles were fairly straightforward. You would pedal up a long gravel road, which intersected with a couple of small creek crossings. The second stretch of road was considerably more challenging. It consisted of a long, winding, downhill grade. There you could expect to find sheer drop-offs two to three hundred feet straight down. All but the most experienced riders were advised to turn back at the summit.

The stunning views in all directions indicated you were at the top of Hurrah Pass. From that point, the road dropped quickly where an added bonus of several oxbows waited in the road. Large boulders frequently tumbled down from landslides, but if luck was still with you by the time you reached the valley floor, you and your bicycle would both still all be in one piece. The right fork of the trail would take you five more miles through deep sandy washes, thirty-degree inclines, and the biggest challenge of all, Jacob's ladder. If you made it this far, you'd have better be prepared to carry your bike up the steepest, most impressive cliff face you've ever attempted. On more than one occasion, it was then that inexperienced mountain bikers realized they had bit off more than they could chew. Most would remember seeing a house being built in the middle of nowhere at the junction of Hurrah Pass and Amasa Back Road. Some of the more observant riders might remember the little gray-and-white dog that trotted down the driveway to greet them.

For many, the small hand-carved wooden sign that said Camelot was confusing. But that sign was the only sign of civilization anywhere around. But by the summer of '99, the little wooden sign would take on a whole new meaning. At all hours of the day and night, bike riders would ride or, in many cases, walk wearily up my driveway. Some were lost, others were out of water, and the rest were just too exhausted to go any farther. I began hauling in extra five-gallon plastic water jugs for those mountain bikers who had heatstroke or were dehydrated, dazed, or confused as to where they were.

Several times each summer, I would have to quit work early to drive the exhausted adventure seekers back to their motel rooms in town. I decided one afternoon it was time to start advertising my future business. Below the Camelot Lodge sign hanging on a post in the driveway, Free Water and Soon To Be Open for Business signs were hung.

The twelve foot tall, two-by-six walls were all framed and standing by spring, but the house was still not livable. I decided to rent a small trailer in a mobile home park during the winter months, so this would be the first time in Jinda's young life where she was not free to roam. It was still possible to paddle the Grumman canoe across the river so I could work on the lodge, but my day job with Paul meant I could only work on Camelot on the weekends. At least twice a month, I would load the old Ford beyond capacity with building supplies. Plywood, studs, doors, and ceiling joist would be roped down then be driven over the steep grade on the back side of the pass. There was one particularly difficult section of the road where some part of my supplies dropped or slid out of the truck.

My progress was agonizingly slow. But after a long day's work, I could always go sit by the river with Jinda. We would lounge on the bank and listen to the birds or gaze up at the sparkling stars in the heavens. There I would remind myself how incredible this place really was.

I finally began to give serious consideration to acquiring my first camel. I would like to start with a young animal, perhaps a female. Ideally, one that had just been weaned. I made a few inquiries with my old friends in the animal-training industry, but they were unaware of anyone with baby camels for sale. One gentleman suggested I contact the lady in Utah who raised camels. This was the most exciting news I had heard in a long time.

The business was listed as Cedar City Camel Ventures. Cedar City, as you may know, is a resort town located about four hours west of Salt Lake. It was the most unusual place to raise or, for that matter, even ride camels. But it was only a few hours away, and their youngest camel was a nine-month-old female with the most perfect name. Lady Gwenievere. After a lengthy phone call with the owner, Shelia White, I scheduled an appointment to drive up to her ranch the following weekend. The unbelievable sequence of events that followed would, in some way, appear to be destiny.

Another angel watching over me? In the not-too-distant future, there would now be a total of three residents in the little secluded valley on the back side of Hurrah Pass: Terry, his faithful dog Jinda, and a wild, rambunctious little camel called Gwennie.

Gwenievere

THE MORNING GWENNIE arrived on the ranch, my customarily quiet, peaceful existence came to a screeching halt. A veteran camel trainer I worked with had warned me years earlier to never trust a black camel, and Gwennie just happened to be about one shade lighter than coal. Still she had a wonderfully adorable personality you just couldn't resist. If the overly curious little beast wasn't getting her head stuck in a bucket, then she was racing up and down the sand dunes, trampling the delicate white petals of the evening primrose or chasing anything that moved. Everything this rambunctious little camel did was a production.

Jinda, for the most part, avoided the meddlesome little troublemaker; but Gwennie had to investigate everything the dog took an interest in. Finally, the safest place to be was anywhere the camel couldn't get to. So Jinda resigned herself to spending the better part of the day lying on the wraparound porch.

*   *   *

Life made sense to my adaptable little dog in Alaska. She had a pretty good handle on bears, especially the black ones. Otis would almost always run. She knew big brown bears should not be approached unless they were in the yard and porcupines had quills longer and sharper than the prickly pear cactus spines and squirrels belonged in the trees. Therein lay the problem. There were no bears around Camelot, but there were plenty of squirrels – big fat garden-robbing squirrels. What was missing, however, were the trees. There were a few cottonwoods along the driveway and some single-leaf ash and coyote willows along the banks of the river, but these squirrels didn't live in trees. They lived in the ground.

Jinda graciously agreed to go along with the new program, so whenever she spotted a squirrel anywhere on the property, she would chase him down a hole. As far as Jinda was concerned, Gwennie was the problem. Her herding abilities worked quite well on the Dalton cattle, but this long-legged critter had feet that flew in all directions and was interrupting her new favorite pastime: chasing ground squirrels.

The moment I walked out the door, I could smell trouble brewing. To the casual observer, everything appeared calm and serene, but that was all about to change. I noticed Gwennie standing in the driveway, investigating a massive anthill, and Jinda was focused on something stirring in the rabbitbrush behind the camel. The rock squirrel was making his way to the bowl of dog food on the porch, unaware his every move was being watched by the intense guard dog. Then three things happened simultaneously that would bring absolute and total chaos to our peaceful little world.

The harvester ants protecting their colony called in the more aggressive larger soldiers to the forefront. At the same time, a dozen ants or more crawled up on Gwennie's tender nose and bit down, the rock squirrel made a dash for the porch toward the dog food, Jinda launched herself directly in the squirrel's path, and all hell broke loose.

Up to this point, Jinda had never actually been kicked by a camel, but that was about to change. Gwennie let out a terrifying roar, causing the plump little rodent to do an about-face and make a beeline for its burrow. The shortest distance between two points is a straight line, and that trajectory would take the scurrying varmint directly beneath the legs of the annoyed young camel. Jinda, not about to let the marauder escape unpunished, dashed headlong through the flailing legs, unaware of the upcoming consequences.

All four feet narrowly missed the fleeing squirrel, but Jinda was not so fortunate. In less than three seconds, the startled little dog was kicked three times and stomped twice. Jinda was outraged. How dare that uncivilized little upstart accost the reigning queen of Camelot? Intending to, once and for all, teach this sassy, ill-mannered camel some manners, Jinda circled behind and nipped Gwennie on the hocks. *Woops!* Turns out camels can kick backward as well.

Finally admitting defeat, the bruised and battered pooch skulked back to the porch to lick her wounds. Gwennie, meanwhile, was still trying to rid herself of the biting ants. Maybe this human could do something besides just stand there as she looked. Before I could make a dash for the safety of the house, Gwennie ran straight toward me. At this point, I was fairly certain that I was about to get trampled; but to my great delight, the frightened animal came to an abrupt halt inches before bone-shattering impact. I began plucking the fiercely biting ants from her nose while she stood frozen in place, moaning pathetically.

Moments later, Gwennie was transformed from a raging devil back to a curious one. Spinning about, she trotted off down the sandy driveway to see what other mischief she could stir up. Jinda was unharmed and, within a few weeks, grew to love the little camel. Most mornings, I would look out in the pasture below the house and see my two companions hunting the elusive rock squirrels. The dog trusted the camel for the most part but remained safely out of reach of the calloused flying feet.

Volumes of short stories could be written about the life and times of Lady Gwenievere, the chocolate-colored camel from Park City. To say the least, life was never boring while in her presence.

The walls of the lodge were now standing, and in a few more weeks, I would have a roof on. I now had the additional responsibility of hauling in hay for my new charge. There was plenty of grazing available, which included tumbleweeds, a favorite closely followed by tamarisk and cottonwood leaves. If she was to grow big and strong enough to carry the throngs of riders who would soon be flocking to southern Utah to ride camels, then she would need proper nutrition, so a daily supplement of hay and grain was provided.

The most time-consuming part of the project was the long trips to town for building supplies. Three hours round-trip before the actual task of nailing it all together. Tourists in rental jeeps and mountain bikes would pass me on the winding road with curious stares. Why in the world was this guy in the beat-up old truck hauling brand-new lumber out into the desert. The ceiling joists for my roof were over thirty feet in length and were draped across the truck from bumper to bumper with fourteen feet dragging behind. Four joists to a load that totals sixty, it would take the better part of a month just to get a roof over my head.

Whenever I made a trip to town, Jinda would ride along. Gwennie figured if her favorite little dog was going anywhere, she was too. The first time I looked in my rearview mirror and saw the half-grown camel trotting behind us, bellowing at the top of her lungs, I realized it was time to build a corral. Paul had a yard full of twisted beams he donated to the cause, and those along with a roll of fencing did the trick. Jinda wasn't too happy about her new buddy being locked up and refused to ride in the truck. Instead, she would lie outside Gwennie's gate and remain there till I returned home and released her captive comrade.

In spite of the incredible amount of work yet to be accomplished, building Camelot and raising Gwennie and Jinda will always be remembered as a highlight in my life. Almost every day, some memorable event occurred, making that day in my life extra special. There was one constant worry. Where was I going to ever find the money to not only pay off the debt I had already incurred, but all the additional funding it would take to furnish the lodge and buy camels.

It was Friday morning, the first week of September. I had yet another meeting with a lending institution that virtually guaranteed me my loan had been approved. I resigned myself to the probability I was once again wasting my time. The only people banks loan money to are those people with large bank accounts who don't really need a loan anyway. Perhaps today would be different. I couldn't give up now.

I arrived ten minutes early; I was always early. Jody used to say I was born in a taxi on the way to the hospital, and I was so obnoxious the cabdriver made us walk the last two miles to the delivery room. When I walked in, the loan specialist, Sarah, was in her office with a middle-aged couple from, of all places, Alaska. Turns out, they weren't there to meet with her, they were waiting for me.

Tom and Nancy met and were married in a small town outside Anchorage. They moved to Moab the year before and looked into purchasing a fifty-acre parcel of land along the banks of the Colorado River about eighteen miles from town. Somebody beat them to it, and that someone was now looking for a loan. Tom dabbled in the stock market, and Nancy bought and sold real estate. Both had been successful in their chosen fields and were now looking to invest in buying land in and around the burgeoning town of Moab.

Tom was about my height, but somewhat stockier. He had a genuine smile, and I liked his honest, straightforward approach.

"So you're the one who bought my land?" he said. He extended his hand, and I accepted the friendly gesture, not knowing who these people were or why they were there. Sarah sat, smiling behind her desk.

"This is Tom and Nancy," she said. "Your loan was rejected, but these folks might be able to help you out. I asked them to come over to meet you."

Nancy stood up from her seat and extended her hand. She was a pleasant-looking woman. Her hair was in a short ponytail, and she was dressed casually in Levi's and a T-shirt. Her well-defined arms and slender build indicated she was no stranger to hard work.

"I have to pick up a few things from the printer," Sarah said. "Why don't you folks make yourselves at home? Sorry about the loan. The lenders felt the property was a little too remote."

Up till know, it hadn't registered my final hurdle might finally be resolved. I was speechless. I was out of options at this point. Every bank, every credit union, and any other lenders I had approached denied my application. Now, out of the blue, there were two people right in front of me ready, I prayed, to give me a loan.

"I can spare about a hundred and twenty-five thousand," Tom said. "The interest is a little higher, but there won't be any closing costs or extra fees."

They had obviously done their homework. All my loan applications had been for the exact amount they had to lend.

"What kind of interest are we talking about?" I asked.

"Ten percent is our standard rate," Nancy said. "We would be first on the title, and you can pay interest only for the first year."

"Why would you make a loan to someone you just met?" I asked.

Tom let out a laugh. "Two reasons," he said. "First, you're from Alaska, and second, you bought some property I had my eye on anyway. If you make your payments, we can always come down and visit you at your ranch. If you don't, you can come down and visit us at our ranch."

The offer was open and honest. There was no doubt about what would become of Camelot if I didn't live up to my end of the bargain, but I also sensed Tom and Nancy sincerely hoped my business would succeed.

"Where do we go from here?" I asked.

Tom opened his satchel and pulled out a simple basic agreement outlining all the terms of the contract. In five minutes, the deal was sealed, and Nancy wrote out a check for the hundred and twenty-five thousand.

"Next time you come to town, we can stop by the title office and take care of the paperwork. If this is a dream, I said don't wake me up now."

I would pay Tom and Nancy back in a year's time, but we would remain friends for a lifetime. From the moment I left Alaska, everything that happened could only be described as good luck. I would need more luck to continue if I was ever going to bring the last crucial piece of the puzzle together. The house and guest rooms were nearly complete. The only things missing were the camels.

Gambling on Camels

BY LATE FALL, the entire shell of the lodge was complete. Of the seven bathrooms, six bathrooms were completely framed, covered in plywood and insulated, then finished in sandstone-colored stucco, and roofed. The basic electrical was in, and all the plumbing was ready for fixtures. The living room with its picturesque eight-foot-by-five-foot window was ready for the final touch.

The old Ford truck was on its last leg, but still running strong. Hauling a ton of Sheetrock in a half-ton truck was about all the old girl could stand. The long, bumpy road was at last taking its toll. The muffler was dangling from the bailing wire where I replaced the broken weld. Both doors sagged, and the bed of the truck was only hanging on by a single rusty bolt. Every trip, I was sure, would be my last; but day after day, mile after grueling mile, the trusty workhorse plugged along.

Paul called one day with some bad news. There were no new jobs coming up in the near future, so I would be temporarily out of work. The good news was he knew a lady in town who was getting rid of an almost-new deluxe woodstove. Tired of shoveling ashes, she would donate the stove to anyone willing to install her new gas model. The unit was massive and would easily heat the entire lodge.

In a matter of hours, we completed the task and, with the assistance of a backhoe, loaded the valuable stove in the truck. Getting it out would nearly be the end of me. Pushing and pulling, grunting and groaning, the thousand-pound unit was moved inch by inch. In the end, it was worth it, though the convenience of flipping a switch to turn on the heat seemed very appealing.

I heard a truck rumbling up the driveway and stepped out on the porch to see who was lost today. To my surprise, it was Gwennie's previous owner, Dr. White. When she exited the vehicle, I noticed that she was limping badly on her right foot.

"What did you do to yourself now?" I asked.

The last time we spoke, she had been kicked by a horse and was disabled for several weeks. Now she was injured again.

"I got thrown off a camel and injured my foot," she said.

Her husband still didn't have a job, and he decided she was going to have to give up the camel business. I remembered the pens being filthy and seeing Clyde, the big bull, standing knee-deep in feces and mud. The other five animals were in no better condition, and I wondered why anyone would keep such valuable animals in such deplorable conditions.

"I've got an offer you are really going to like," she said.

I invited her in to listen to her proposition. After taking her on the fifty-cent tour of the house, we stepped back out on the porch for a cold drink.

"Listen, I know you would like to start up your camel business soon, and I am way too busy at work to take care of all the animals – "

I stopped her there. "I haven't been able to get a loan on the house," I said. "No one is going to loan me money on a bunch of camels."

She nodded her head in understanding.

"Hear me out," she replied. "I've invested about a hundred thousand in my business including the camels, the truck and trailer, the saddles, and all the camping equipment and the corrals. What would you think if I was to offer the entire package for an interest in Camelot?"

When something sounds too good to be true, it usually is, but she definitely had my attention.

"Why not just sell the business outright?" I asked.

"The property gains tax would cost me a fortune, and I could never get what the animals are worth. Roger thinks the camels are too much work, and now I've been thrown he really just wants to get rid of them. When would I have to pay you for everything? This was when I expected to get the bad news. You won't have to pay a dime until you sell the lodge," she said.

"I might never sell the place, and you'll be out all that money."

"This would be a better home for the camels," she said. "And I can concentrate on my business."

I sensed this was not her idea, but I had to agree. The animals would be much happier in the desert where they belonged, and Gwennie would love to have some camel company.

"You can come out and ride anytime you like," I said.

We worked out the details for the transfer of ownership. Dr. White and her lazy husband, Roger, would own one-third of the real estate at Camelot, but I would own the camel-trekking business and all the equipment that went along with it.

"By the way," she said. "You also get free veterinary care from the top camel vet in the country."

"Who is that?" I asked.

"Me, of course." And she left.

That question I had earlier about something too good to be true suddenly flashed before my eyes. Why would someone who knew everything about animal husbandry have kept animals in such awful conditions?

"We have a deal," I said.

Park City Camel Ventures would now be known as Canyonlands Camel Ventures, and Dr. White would be the proud new owner of sixteen acres of prime land in the beautiful valley of Hurrah Pass, Utah.

The Camels Are Coming:
The Ride Home

A REPORTER FROM the local newspaper arrived early. The story about the camels' arrival to Moab would be featured on front page. Moab was already well-known for its stunning scenery, world-class mountain biking, two national parks, and multiday excursions on the Colorado River; but no one had ever offered camel treks here before.

Because of the rugged road, a custom-built stock trailer was not an option. We would have to ride the camels into the lodge property. Several people from town volunteered to help, but none had ever ridden anything except a horse.

My stomach was in knots. There were numerous obstacles along the way, which included traffic, five-hundred-foot drop-offs, hairpin turns, and a bunch of anxious greenhorns ready to ride the range on ships of the desert.

Gordon, the driver transporting the camels from Park City, arrived an hour later than scheduled; and the sun was already heating things up. About the time the reporter was ready to pack it in, a long trailer followed by a cloud of dust came barreling around the corner.

I could tell by his surly disposition, our driver was thoroughly annoyed at having to drive the camels to Moab. He stepped out of the big one-ton truck and began barking out orders. The volunteers were taken aback. Who was this bag of hot air showing up late and then mad at everyone else? I was too excited to give it much thought.

The first camel out was Cefa. I had truly never seen such a gorgeous camel in my life. Her golden coat was long and silky, and her gentle demeanor caused everyone to take a deep breath and relax. Keith and Lori approached first. They were already acquainted with Gwennie, but by comparison, Cefa was an absolute angel.

Next out of the trailer was Moto. The name was short for motor boat, and the moment he was secured to the trailer by a lead rope, he let out a long *blub-blub-blub-blub-blub.*

"Sounds like a forty-horse outboard," someone remarked.

"That's just his way of saying hello," Mary said. Mary had worked with the camels in Park City, and Moto was her absolute favorite.

The first thing everyone noticed about this animal, besides his enormous size, was his long, luxurious eyelashes. Moto, indeed, had lashes that would make a Maybelline model envious. There was never a more agreeable animal alive. Moto loved two things in life, people and carrots, and we had plenty of both. Mary immediately began brushing Moto down so he could be saddled.

The Wonderfull Wild Bill

Raji, Cefa's mom, was next to exit. When she stepped out into the sunlight, she immediately called to her daughter. The two animals were tied up side by side. Raji was darker than her offspring and appeared to be a little anxious. But within a few minutes, she calmed down and began to chew her cud.

The last camel to emerge from the stock trailer was Curly. If ever there was a camel that could not be trusted, it was Curly. He had a long history of bucking people off and running over anyone in his path.

"Looks like I will be riding Curly," I said. He and I might as well get things established now. I would be the rider, and he would be the "ridee." At least, I hoped that's how it would go. Clyde, the bull camel, and Bill, one of my favorites, would be picked up next week because for now, we had our hands full.

I decided to saddle Cefa up for the newspaper story. She settled into the cached position (all legs folded beneath her recusant body) while I groomed her and placed the custom-made leather saddle on her back. The girth and chest straps were cinched in place, and soon we were ready for our rider. But it wasn't certain whether he was ready for us or not.

The color in the reporter's cheeks looked a little pale, and even with some reassuring coaxing, he wasn't about to budge. Mary came to the rescue by slipping her toe in the stirrup and throwing her leg over the opposite side.

"Hut," she said, and Cefa rose to her feet gracefully.

"Nothing to it," I added.

"Okay," the reporter said. "I'll give it a try."

He stayed in the saddle just long enough to snap a couple of pictures and then was more than ready to dismount. Our first official camel rider in Moab would evidently not be our most willing.

As we saddled the remaining camels, the reporter fired off several questions for the article. Within an hour, both he and Gordon departed, leaving our small party of wannabe camel wranglers mounted and ready for the long trek to the lodge.

Filming Wild New World At CAmelot The B.B.C crew

Everything went surprisingly well that afternoon. Even Curly behaved himself. For the first hour, the riders chatted away. Most commented on how smooth the ride was and how relaxing it was to ride a camel. On the second half of the trip, however, things began to change and the complaining started. By the time we reached Hurrah Pass, an hour and a half from where the excursion began, everyone but Keith was ready to get off and walk. That was probably a good idea since the twists and turns in the road on the back side of the pass would make even the most seasoned riders nervous, and these were amateur riders at best. Lori, one of the riders, had thankfully brought chicken and drinks for the group. While the camels nibbled on tamarisk and tumbleweeds, we took a short lunch break in the shade.

The sandstone cliffs dwarfed the small caravan as we made our way down the twisting trail. When the lodge eventually came into sight, our pace began to pick up. I am uncertain as to whether the animals sensed this was their new home or if Gwennie's constant bellowing peaked their interest. She had been left at the lodge, and they could hear her. As we rounded the final bend, Curly, Raji, Moto, and Cefa became anxious at the familiar call and focused their attention locating its source.

Jinda, who had remained at home to babysit Gwennie, heard us coming and rushed down the road to greet the saddle-sore troop. All of the camels but one paid no heed to the frisky dog. Curly predictably began hopping and jumping in grand "camel fashion," causing everyone around him to panic and run for cover. Fortunately, the tantrum only lasted a matter of seconds; so as quickly as it had begun, peace was once more promptly restored for the weary band of travelers.

After the saddles were removed and the animals were thoroughly brushed, we released them into the five-acre pasture to graze. At first, the animals just stood in a group, uncertain of what to do. It donned on me these animals had never before experienced freedom. Moto was the first to begin exploring his new home. He sniffed the various plants in the new enclosure and tentatively sampled the tufts of rice grass and tumbleweed. Soon all the camels were racing around the pasture like schoolkids at recess.

The group of volunteers retired to the lodge for a well-deserved rest and a cold drink. Most admitted the long trek was more difficult than they had imagined, but it was one of the greatest adventures of their life. Mary was saddened by the fact that her beloved Moto would be so far away. But over the next two years, she would make numerous trips to Camelot to visit her gangly friend. She would always be a welcome guest at Camelot, and Moto would not forget her.

Early the next morning, I dashed into town for a copy of the morning paper. As promised, Franklin Seal's story made front page. There sat the terrified wide-eyed reporter atop beautiful Cefa with the caption THE CAMELS ARE COMING! It was now final. The camels were here, and Camelot Adventure Lodge was officially open for business.

The Eyes Have It

Moto

EACH MORNING, I would awake at first light and venture down the camel pens to check my new family. After a quick breakfast of grass hay and grain, the camels were moved to the pasture to graze and stretch their legs. Curly was usually the instigator of any early-morning mischief. After circling the rest of the animals, he would usually hop in place then dash around the open field with feet flying in all directions. Raji and Cefa would huddle together, waiting for the antics to cease. Moto was unimpressed with the bronco routine and would stand his ground, blubbering a warning.

I became concerned the two animals may eventually injure one another, so on my next trip into town, I contacted Dr. White to ask her opinion as to whether there was any cause for alarm or not.

"No," she assured me. "Curly is all bluff. The two animals had lived together for years, and they seem to get along fine."

It would be the first bad advice the good doctor would give me regarding the welfare of the camel herd. Unfortunately, it would eventually result in a serious injury to Moto as well as a lack of trust with the troublemaking Curly. After the article in the paper, the residents of Moab began to show up at all hours of the day. They were curious about the new and unusual business that had opened near their town.

The reactions varied from surprise such as "I didn't even know there was a road out here" to amusing comments such as "Why in the world would anyone drive all the way out here to ride a dang camel." My progress on the lodge was being hindered by the constant intrusions, but these were potential guests as well as new friends, so they were always treated with great respect. By this time, I was hanging Sheetrock, and most of the living room and master bedroom were nearly finished. Soon I could begin finalizing construction on the guest rooms. I would have to stop working whenever a truck pulled into the driveway. I would take the visitors down to meet the camels. This was usually followed up with the nickel tour of the guest lodge.

Moto-boat would always get the most attention next to Gwennie. He never failed to emit his namesake greeting. The blubbering call would typically result in a good laugh. Although some visitors found his habit a bit unnerving. Dr. White decided to drive out to Camelot one afternoon to check on her investment. She agreed to bring the two remaining camels with her, relieving me from having to put in the long five-hour drive to pick them up on my own.

I had forgotten how huge Clyde was. When the big bull Clyde came out of the trailer, it almost seemed as if the leaf springs on the rig bounced back into the customary half-moon position. His extremely large head was the most noticeable thing about the beast. Unlike Moto and the rest of the animals whose hair was long and straight, Clyde's fur was tightly curled on his immense frame. His color was taffy brown, and he carried himself with the stature of nobility. Everything about this regal animal exuded leadership and confidence. His previous living conditions were less than sanitary, so his muscular legs and chest were caked in dried mud and feces.

This camel, I vowed, would never live in such filth again. Life at Camelot would be a better existence for all the animals. Here they would receive love and the extra attention they needed to thrive. But first, we would have to get them home. I remembered Bill being the tallest of the group. But I had forgotten how elegant he looked. Although not nearly as stocky as Clyde, he was a head taller. I was surprised he could stand upright in the custom trailer.

The moment he emerged, I was awestruck. If Clyde was to be the King Arthur of Camelot, then Bill would be Lancelot. Anyone who ever described camels as unattractive had never laid eyes on this bunch of animals. Well, okay, Clyde wasn't exactly what you might describe as glamorous, but he did have a certain rugged John Wayne kind of attractiveness to him. At least, Cefa and Raji thought so.

We saddled up the last two members of the herd, and for the second time in a week, we began the long, arduous ride over the pass. I hoped this would be the last time the camels would travel over this dangerous, rocky road. All seven camels could now settle down to a quiet existence in the home of their long-departed ancestors. Dr. White spent that night and most of the following day reliving stories of her recent camel adventures, which included a trip to Australia, a tour in Dubai, and visits to the camel ranches stateside. The stories all shared a common theme: frustration.

"If only they would listen to my advice," she would say, "things would be so much better."

Sadly, I felt if only she would have listened to their advice, her faltering camel business would have thrived with far fewer mistakes and far fewer accidents. Fortunately, most of these camels were still young animals and could be easily retrained. My own somewhat-limited experience with camels was under the supervision of a gentleman by the name of Bill Rivers. He is, without a doubt, one of the most talented and well-recognized hoof-stock trainers in the country. He was never too busy to lend a helping hand or give a word of advice to a previous student.

Bill's camels appeared in numerous films and commercials, so my early years as a trainer were greatly enhanced with his guidance. The infamous Dr. White departed the next day with final words of advice that thankfully I would not be required to follow. I could only pray her medical expertise far exceeded her extremely limited training experience. The lives of my camels would depend on it.

Moto wasted little time establishing himself as second in command under Clyde. The powerful bull would take the throne as reigning king of Camelot while Moto would become known as the camel with the biggest heart. Over the next two years, Moto proved to be one of the most trustworthy and lovable camel I had ever known. He suffered a tragic and needless injury when he was brutally attacked by Curly though. The spinal fracture left Moto paralyzed, which required the wonderful animal to be euthanized. Dr. White arrived with an electric cattle prod and a fatal dose of serum.

"Kill him or cure him!"

Moto succumbed to the treatment as expected. He died in fear.

It would be the last time Dr. White treated any of my animals. Unfortunately for Cefa and Moto, my decision would come too late.

The Legend of Wild Bill

A S THE LONG, hot days of summer dragged on, the monsoon rains had not yet arrived, which typically brought relief to the drought-stricken desert. The leaves of the wild rhubarb, which only a few weeks earlier appeared lush and green, were now wilted and brown.

I began my walk at first light for good reason. Within a few short hours, the blazing sun would raise the temperatures to almost-unbearable level. Bill cantered to the gate, eager to join the excursion. He frequently accompanied me on my early-morning jaunts while the rest of the small band of animals lay in the cushed position, contentedly chewing their cud.

Gwennie, the youngest of the herd, stood briefly as if to consider joining the trek by stretching her long and muscular legs. She then neck-folded her legs, jack-knife fashion, and settled back into the resting position.

I swung the rusty metal gate open, and Bill politely waited for me to pass before exiting the pasture. The massive animal towered over me. His shoulders were almost head high to me, making it easy to reach the leaves beyond the ten-foot mark on the Fremont cottonwood. At nearly a ton in weight, his gentle demeanor was exceptional even for camels. I knew little of his background. The previous owner guessed his age at around eleven or twelve years. Bill was raised in Southern California on a ranch that supplied animals for the motion picture industry. His only credits were a short scene in the movie *Independence Day*. The shot was of two camels lying outside a tent in Iran (actually filmed in Las Vegas) as a giant spaceship passes overhead, which luckily required no acting ability.

The reason for him being sold was never disclosed. Perhaps financial difficulties or the previous owner was intimidated by his great size. Whatever the reasons, I considered myself blessed to have acquired this noble stead. As I reached into my pack to retrieve an apple, Bill lowered his great head to investigate. I stroked his silky muzzle and gently scratched his sloping forehead.

"Do you think I brought this for you?" I said, holding it up in the palm of my hand. I extended my arm, inviting Bill to take his share of the fruit. He quickly wrapped his long prehensile lips around the treat and chomped down, severing the apple in half. What remained suddenly looked very unappetizing, so I pinched the other half between my fingers and raised it above my head, offering it as well.

We followed the road for several hundred yards, stopping occasionally to examine a footprint in the soft pink sand. Fox and coyote tracks were common as well as desert bighorn sheep as they frequently crossed the road on their way to the river to quench their thirst. Bill plodded along behind me, camel-style. He showed little interest in the tracks but would nibble on the withering tufts of rice grass growing between the slate gray sagebrush.

By necessity, most mammals in the desert are nocturnal. Merriam's kangaroo rats, white-footed deer mice, and other rodents emerged only after dark as they often fell victims to the wily kit fox. Leaving the road, we worked our way down a steep sand dune to a long winding arroyo at the base of the cliffs. Our browsing would be better from there, and relief from the already-scorching rays of the sun could be sought in the lingering shadows of the steep sandstone walls. Camels are unaffected by the stifling heat. Nature endowed these creatures with the ability to thermoregulate. That is, to raise or lower their body temperature according to the weather. As protection from the winter cold, Bill's dense winter coat could also insulate his body from the heat of the summer sun. The dense wool was, in fact only now, beginning to shed from his huge frame.

We made our way toward a large cluster of boulders in the center of an open meadow. Locals referred to it as Catacomb Rock, a series of natural caves permeating the unusual formation. The temperature was considerably cooler within the caverns, and a small seep in the larger cave would give the always-thirsty camel a sip of water.

Toward the east, the sun crested over the thousand-foot cliffs, instantly raising the air temperature to an uncomfortable ninety-plus degrees. A black-tailed jackrabbit bolted from his lair beneath the Mormon tea and zigzagged through the brush. Without warning, he suddenly leaped high into the air, announcing the direction of his erratic travels. Bill seemed unimpressed by the acrobatic display and instead opted to investigate a brightly colored lizard basking on a flat slab of shale. The dark black ring around this reptile's neck identified it as a collared lizard. His bold blue-green head bobbed a warning to the inquisitive camel, but realizing the threat did not have its desired effect, the robust lizard decided instead to dart into a nearby crevice.

As we climbed out of the brush-choked ravine onto the rolling dunes, there was a faint though distinct hum of engines echoed throughout the previously serene valley. The annoying sound of ATVs approaching in the distance was a sign our peaceful morning excursion would soon end. Typically, the noisy four-wheeled machines avoided my secluded valley, preferring instead to wreak their havoc on the creek bottoms nearer to town. The increase in popularity over the past few years in the open rangelands of Southern Utah made intrusions like this more and more common. Moab was obviously now a favorite destination for the new fast-paced generation of backcountry explorers and riders. From far and wide, they converged on the once-quiet tourist town to race across the hundreds of miles of dirt roads at breakneck speeds. A few riders were considerate of those in their path; but sadly, most sped across the desert landscape in reckless abandon, choking fellow travelers in a thick cloud of dust.

There was much work to be done at the ranch before the sun reached its zenith, so I convinced myself to head back in the direction of the lodge and explore the wind caves on another outing. Bill chose to travel down the dried riverbed while I climbed to the road above, though we were both heading home in the same direction. What little grazing still available to the hungry camel was more likely to be found in the cooler canyon floor.

As I rounded the corner on the narrow serpentine road, I could make out the silhouette of two riders approaching in the distance, perhaps a mile away. As always, a long plume of dust and haze followed in their wake. Maybe with activity, I should join Bill in the bottom of the ravine, but that would entail climbing up the steep hillside once the riders had passed. No, I decided, I would have to eat a little dust, which was to be expected whenever a vehicle passed by.

With the house and barn tucked in a side canyon neatly out of site, the two riders had no idea a guest lodge even existed out here. If they spotted the camel, then they would really be confused.

A few hundred yards before they rounded the bend, both motorcycles suddenly came to an abrupt stop. The men dismounted and walked a few steps back down the road. One of them removed his helmet and kneeled down on the deep sand as if about to receive communion or perhaps asking permission to be granted knighthood. As I got closer, the gentleman still standing looked up in my direction. A lone traveler on foot in the middle of the desert usually meant only one thing, and his first question confirmed his incorrect assumption.

"Where's you're truck?" he asked.

"I left it home," I answered.

"You walked all the way out here?"

I considered explaining to my concerned new friend my house was just over the next rise; but before I could do so, the second man rose to his feet, and a flurry of new questions erupted.

"Do you need some water? How long have you been out here? Do you want a ride back to town?"

I started to chuckle. "I'm fine," I said. "I come out here all the time."

"You do?" the previously kneeling man said. "Well, maybe you could help answer a question for me."

"What is it?" I said as he pointed to the large dinner plate-sized tracks in the sand. I knew what the curiosity was all about.

"Do you have any idea what made these unusual tracks in the road?" he asked, looking down the ground.

The two strangers hadn't noticed the lumbering giant in the ravine below. Bill, having given up on the prospect of any worthwhile breakfast being located in the dry wash, climbed up the road to investigate the commotion on the road. Both men had their backs to the large beast as he approached, and I couldn't resist the temptation to play a harmless prank on the two unsuspecting victims. I looked down at the giant footprints crossing the road. Scratching my chin in an apparent attempt to solve the riddle, I decided to throw out a few suggestions.

"Couldn't be cows," I said.

"Too big to be a horse," one man added.

By this time, Bill was standing only a few feet behind the men, and the time had come to spring the trap. I raised my arms in the air as if the mystery of the giant footprints had suddenly been revealed to me.

"I know what made those tracks!" I said.

Both men asked in unison, "What?" Bill was now practically resting his chin on their helmets.

"Those are wild camel tracks," I said.

"Wild camels?" A broad smile spread across their faces.

"There aren't any camels in Utah," exclaimed the man who was closest to Bill.

"Really," I said. "That one behind you has been following me around out here for the last three hours."

In total disbelief, both men rolled their eyes. But nonetheless, they turned in the direction I was pointing. No words could describe the look on the men's faces as they spun in their tracks and bolted in the direction of the only possible escape available. The motorcycles were still sputtering in the road. Hopefully, the bikes would save them from the fire-breathing dragon, which had silently emerged from the depths of hell.

"Get on," one man said as he stomped down on the gears and began fleeing down the road.

It's probably a good thing I wasn't being attacked by a pack of rabid wolves, I thought. Any hope for rescue was now fleeing down the road at top speed. I laughed out loud and headed at a brisk pace across the desert in the direction of the house. Only after escaping to a safe distance did both men look back and realize they had been duped. Pointing their finger in my direction, shaking their heads, they both began to laugh. Any friends or family waiting for them back at camp would probably find their wild tale somewhat suspect. But their wild adventure that hot August morning would never be forgotten.

Later that day, I heard the familiar sound of motorcycles coming up the driveway. I peered out the kitchen window at two riders. I poured two tall glasses of cold lemonade as a peace offering as the men climbed off the bikes and turned off the engines. They briefly stopped to stare out at the six camels grazing in their pens. I could hear them laughing about the events that had transpired earlier in the day. Opening the door, I stepped out on the porch with a glass in each hand. The men accepted the cold drink with a thank-you.

"You got me," the taller of the two said.

His friend nodded his head in agreement. I led them to a bench on the long shaded porch and invited them to sit. As we sat there in the shade, a light breeze blew a dust devil down the driveway, and I shared the story of Camelot with my two new friends. Although they never took me up on my offer to join me on a camel ride, the two men would visit me every summer. They would often bring along a witness to corroborate the stories they told about the wild camels in the deserts of Utah.

From then on and without exception, there was always a bag of apples in their cooler for the animals. The biggest apple was always set aside, hand-washed, and polished for their favorite camel of all: a ten-foot-tall gentle giant by the name of Wild Bill.

Cefa, My Favorite Angel

GENETICS IS A strange process. Combine one rugged, stout bull with one average-looking walnut brown female; and thirteen months later, out pops the most silky, gorgeous baby camel you've ever seen. Every aspect of Cefa spelled elegance. From her gentle and trusting personality to her striking color, Cefa was special. Some would argue these traits might be better used to describe creatures like horses, big cats, or a handsome impala. Elegant was a title bestowed on certain breeds of dogs, but camels? Never.

If you looked close at the soft, liquid brown eyes, then you could see they were surrounded by long luxurious lashes. Run your fingers through the dense, smooth undercoat or stroke the silken muzzle. Only then will you too develop a deeper appreciation for these remarkable animals.

It's true I am somewhat biased, but having worked with camels for almost a decade, I cannot help but admire what the cameleers in 1856 referred to as the Noble Brutes. Most visitors to Camelot would spend an extra moment or two gazing at Cefa. Those who came to ride often requested her. Perhaps her smaller stature or her inviting look set them at ease. After the trek, there was endless praise. Her gait was, by far, the smoothest; and she never attempted to hop or run back to the barn. To sum it all up, Cefa was a lady.

She lived with me for only a year, but it would be a camel I would never forget. Try as I might to not show favoritism, it was she who first came to mind whenever I thought about going on an early-morning ride. Most camels prefer to go in a group, but Cefa seemed to enjoy the solo outings and never hesitated to travel alone.

*   *   *

So you wonder: how do you steer a camel? It was one of the most common questions asked at the lodge, but there was more than one answer to that question. Because camels chew their cud, you cannot put a bit in their mouth as you would a horse. These camels came retrofitted with nose plugs. The reins attach to the plug with a nylon line and are then fed through a ring on either side of a leather harness clipped around the camel's chest. This apparatus is commonly referred to as a running martingale and is used to steer or stop. Verbal commands are also used to direct the animals. Hush means lie down. Hut to stand and walk up or start moving. Cefa would always respond to the gentlest tug or the softest whisper.

*   *   *

In the spring of 2000, I walked down the pasture to feed and water the camels. They all met me at the gate for any special treats I may be hiding in my pockets. I noticed that Cefa was missing her nose plug. Like everything, the plastic plugs would eventually wear out and break off. I contacted Dr. White to find out where I could order a new plug, and she graciously offered to drive out in the next few weeks to help me replace it since the camels were also due for their annual vaccinations. It would be a tragic mistake that I would deeply regret. When Dr. White arrived, there was obvious tension in the air. She was often worried usually about money. Her husband was unemployed but insisted on having nice things like a new truck, a custom jeep, flying lessons, or a sports car. Dr. White worked constantly to pay the bills while the husband stayed home, spending the money. I often wondered what she saw in the lazy man, but that was not my affair, so we avoided the topic.

"Let's do Cefa first," she said.

I had never installed a nose plug, so I was eager to see how it was done. I went to put a halter on Cefa while Dr. White got everything ready. Her husband headed for the porch with a cooler to sit in the shade.

"Don't you want to help?" she asked as he was walking away.

"No, you two can handle it," he said, not bothering to turn around.

What a waste, I thought. When I looked back at Dr. White, she was drawing up a syringe full of clear liquid. I assumed the substance in the syringe was Cefa's annual vaccination.

"This will take the edge off," she said. It was at that point I realized the doctor had administered some sort of sedative.

"Is that necessary to replace a nose plug?" I asked.

"I'm not looking to get kicked," she replied. "And we may have to enlarge the hole."

Cefa began to get groggy almost immediately. She stood with her feet spread wide and her head hanging nearly to the ground. Something didn't feel right, and Dr. White became concerned as well.

"How much did I inject?" she said.

I had no idea, but the statement made me feel queasy inside.

"Is something wrong?" I asked.

"No," she said. "She'll be okay." As Cefa lowered herself to the ground, Dr. White reached into the truck for a new nose plug. Slipping the small end first into the nostril, she pushed with considerable force, popping the end of the knob out through the small opening. Cefa let out a faint groan.

"That's all there is to it," she said.

"How long until she comes out of the anesthesia?" I asked.

Her reluctance to reply told me something was terribly wrong.

This woman is a licensed veterinarian, I told myself. *Surely she knows what she is doing*. It took more than an hour for Cefa to regain her footing, but her head was still hung down, and her eyes were dull and nearly lifeless.

Dr. White drew up six vaccinations and quickly injected all the camels but Cefa.

"We have to get back," she said and began walking toward the house.

"Don't you think you should stick around till Cefa's better?" I asked.

"No," she insisted. "I'll call you when we get home. Just keep an eye on her."

When they got back in the truck, I could hear her husband complaining about the drive home. Dr. White smiled briefly, but the look on her face told me Cefa wasn't responding well to the shot and there wasn't anything she could do to help. By the time the truck made it to the top of Hurrah Pass, a small trickle of blood was seeping down the camel's nose. By the time Dr. White returned to her home, the trickle had increased to a steady flow.

"She must have had a reaction to the anesthetic," she said when I told her about the bleeding.

"Call me tomorrow if there is no improvement."

But for the helpless camel, tomorrow would never come. My beautiful Cefa was dying, and no amount of praying would prevent it. I brought her to the house and tied her to the hitching post in the front yard. Her condition continued to worsen, and by the time the sun was beginning to set, she could no longer lift her head from the ground. I retrieved a sleeping bag from the house and lay next to her on the ground. The other camels began to call out for her, but she was too weak to answer.

"I am so sorry," I said as I stroked her soft muzzle. Sometime around midnight, Cefa took her last raspy breath. Her head lay down in the soft sand, and her big brown eyes closed for the final time. I began to sob uncontrollably. Out loud, I asked God, "Why do you bring such pain on your children?" I heard no reply.

Cefa was buried on a small knoll overlooking the pasture. On a flat slab of sandstone, I engraved her name and three short words, YOU WERE LOVED. Jinda followed me around the yard the following morning. She too grieved the loss of

Cefa. The rest of the camels continued calling for their missing sister, but by nightfall, they too realized she would not be coming back.

It was months before I could bring myself to ride again, but it was Bill who eventually brought me around. I walked out of the house one morning and found him lying next to Cefa's grave. He too was saying his final goodbye. Dr. White never spoke of the incident again. Although in her heart she felt responsible for the tragic death of Cefa, it was too costly a mistake to acknowledge. Eventually, things returned to normal at Camelot, and the beautiful young camel that brought so much joy to all would always be remembered.

Mighty Clyde

Mighty Clyde

Saddling Clyde for another great trek

A SHORT TIME after the camels had arrived, I received a very exciting phone call. The gentleman on the other end identified himself as a producer/director with BBC.

The company was currently working on a six-part documentary titled *Wild New World*. The program was a depiction of prehistoric North America and would reenact the early people and animals that existed on this continent at the end of the last Ice Age. Most of the mammals had to be replicated on a computer. Saber-toothed cats, mastodons, giant ground sloths, and short-faced bears are all extinct now; but one mammal, although no longer living wild in North America, still exists.

Camels, in record numbers, once roamed the open grasslands of North America when nomadic people first crossed the Bering Strait. These and other ungulates were undoubtedly hunted for food and clothing. It has even been suggested that camels were hunted to near extinction by humans.

Moab would be a perfect backdrop for the series, and my camels would have starring roles. John, the producer for the show, flew into Salt Lake City the following week to survey the surrounding area and go over some of the scenes. He also inquired if I might be willing to dress up in some caveman garb and run around the desert, chasing camels with a spear. This looked very promising for my struggling new business venture, and I could barely contain my excitement. The best part was the film crew would also need accommodations. If I could finish the lodge in time, they would lease out all the rooms including meals. The future was looking very bright indeed.

John and his assistant, Paul (perfect names for a couple of guys from England), arrived on schedule and rented a four-wheel-drive vehicle to travel down to Camelot. I worked feverishly to get the guest rooms completed prior to their arrival. Sinks, showers, and carpeting were hastily installed; and the final coat of paint was being applied on the morning they drove to the property.

The two men were overwhelmed by the incredible scenery surrounding them. Equally exciting was the small herd of camels wandering along the hillside. If they had brought along a camera, then they would have probably begun filming that very instant. I assured them everything would be finished at the lodge when they returned in the fall, so the deal was sealed. When Clyde wandered down to say hello, I could tell they were understandably cautious, perhaps even a little intimidated by the great lumbering brute. They were anxious to see the surrounding desert landscape, so why not do it on the back of a camel, I suggested. The two men were elated at the prospect of riding the camels into the backcountry, so after a quick lunch, we saddled up three camels and off we went.

Clyde would, of course, lead the trek; and Bill and Moto would follow behind. The weather could not have been more perfect. Without another soul around, we enjoyed a clear blue sky with a light breeze from the west. The moment we cleared the first tall sand dune, both riders gasped in amazement.

"It was as if," John said, "we had just stepped back in time two hundred and fifty thousand years."

We rode for several hours, looking at various rock formations, exploring hidden canyons, and gazing down the winding river below. The two filmmakers were ecstatic with the prospect of filming the first segment of their project here. But weary and saddle sore, we dismounted and sat on a bluff overlooking the mighty Colorado, discussing some of the shots. We all agreed that Clyde would be the star of the show. His grizzled coat, large head, and girth combined with his other prehistoric features reeked with the title of the film. I suggested we change the name to *Clyde's Wild New World*. The name change didn't stick.

However, impressions made by the camels and the scenery did. Before leaving the ranch, a contract was signed and a hefty deposit check was written out to Camelot Adventure Lodge. I would have less than sixty days to finish the house, locate the trainers, and hire a cook. Whatever lack of sleep I was getting up to this point was about to get cut in half. You asked for it, I told myself, as John and Paul headed back to town. The first official camel trekkers were on their way back to England, and the first movie deal at Camelot was signed and sealed. In spite of extreme exhaustion and a thrilling new future, I would have no trouble sleeping that night.

*　　　*　　　*

"Lights, camera, action!" I said to my camels as I tucked them all into bed. "You are the greatest."

The day after the final touches were applied to the lodge that included curtains, pictures, and running water, the film crew arrived. Heavy clouds hung in the air, and it looked like the monsoon season had arrived. I was thinking disaster, but they were fine with the rain. We sat down at the newly constructed kitchen table. Eighteen-foot-long two-by-twelves with stout four-by-six legs. The table would seat ten and fit nicely in front of the picture window looking over the river.

*　　　*　　　*

Now, there's one thing you should know about most production companies. They always have a budget. It's like Congress. They pull some arbitrary figure out of the hat and swore up and down there would be no way they can afford the price you quoted them. But I had learned from the master.

Nick Toth, from Cougar Hill, knew exactly how to get the price you needed to make it work. Find the scene they can't live without, and make it the most difficult shot of all. Then reel them in. Paul and John worked the "good cop, bad cop" routine well, so I waited for the right moment to make up the dollar amount we differed on.

"Listen, Terry," John said. "Is there a way to train a camel to lie on his side like he has just been killed?"

There it was. All those deals I made earlier in the negotiations were about to get a dramatic raise. It wasn't really dishonest – it was just business.

"Camels do occasionally lie on their side," I said. "But to train a camel to do it can be very difficult and dangerous. It would take some time. I would say about a week to ten days."

"We couldn't go more than a week," John said. "What would that cost?"

I quickly calculated everything involved, money wise, then multiplied it by two and wrote down the figure on the budget sheet. Paul's eyes rolled back in his head like he had just been possessed by a demon.

"That is twice the amount what we would be able to justify for that shot. We may have to delete the scene," John said. They both looked in my direction.

"You know what? Since you're booking the entire lodge for a week and paying to rent all six camels, I guess I could come down about a third on the price. If I can't get the shot, I'll deduct the training from your final bill."

The two men smiled at one another, and I'm certain I saw John wink to his partner. Now if I could just get Clyde to not flop down on his side the moment the rain let up, then I might be able to pull this off. Clyde, you see, loved nothing more than a good roll in the sand whenever his wool got wet. He usually thrashed around in the dirt like he was in his final death throes. I planned to move him out of sight until the day of the shoot and amaze the two English gentlemen with my remarkable ability to train camels. They will get their final shot for the film, and I would be back on budget. My budget, not theirs.

The filming began the next morning. Most of the shots were quite simple – camels standing around, grazing in the desert. Not something you really have to train them to do. Mary, a friend from Park City, came down to help out. Any opportunity to hang out with her favorite camel Moto needed little persuasion. Throw in a paycheck, and she'll even show up on time.

Clyde was, without a doubt, declared most valuable player. Whenever a scene came up that required an animal that never spooked, it would be Clyde. Now camels, by nature, are usually unfazed by things that would make a horse go ballistic. Be it cavemen running at them with spears or cameras rushing up from behind them in the tall grass. Strong winds ripping the roof off their hay barn had little to no effect on the animals even when it dropped it a few yards away. It made no difference when a group of motorcycles went racing by. The camels remained calm. Clyde wouldn't even raise his head in their direction.

*　　　*　　　*

The day came at last. The big conclusion: Clyde's death scene. The two men had been grilling me all week on how the training was going, and I responded with a positive outlook.

"We're 90 percent there," I said.

The summer sun was beating down in full force when we led Clyde to the river's edge. The exposed sandbar would make a great back place to exfoliate the burly camel. Paul manned the camera while John went over the shot.

He said, "A saber-toothed cat will follow the camels to the river and is creeping through the grass. Without warning, he rushes forward and jumps on the camel, knocking him to the ground. Clyde has to thrash around like he's been attacked. Ten or twelve seconds should do it. What do you think?"

I walked up to Clyde and whispered in his ear like a coach rehearsing the lines for Hamlet. "He's ready, roll camera," I said.

Mary played her part perfectly.

"Terry, do you think we should cool Clyde down before he lies down in the sand?"

I felt the sand with my hand to check the temperature. "Yeah," I said. "Wouldn't hurt. Grab that grain bucket and pour some water over his hump too."

Mary did as instructed, soaking Clyde's dense wool and dumping the remainder of the water on the sand around his feet. Clyde shook briefly, and just as the camera began to roll, I whispered the secret command to the veteran actor.

"Bullshit," I said quietly. Clyde looked in my direction, and I repeated the order, "Bullshit."

Clyde's front legs buckled, then his rear legs folded under his belly. With a great groan, the one-ton bull flopped to his side and began flailing his legs in ecstasy. Sand was flying in all directions, and Clyde's long lips were flapping like a flag in a whirlwind at half-mast. At long last, Clyde, having thoroughly scratched his muscular back, threw his long neck out in a great arch and closed his eyes to relax in the warm, wet sand. The camera continued to roll, and both men appeared to be holding their breath. Finally, Clyde righted himself and shook the sand from his dripping wet coat.

"Brilliant, bloody brilliant," said John.

Paul strode forward to congratulate me on the excellent training that had resulted in the perfect shot. While he shook my hand with great exuberance, he asked me what command I used to teach the difficult behavior.

"If I tell you, I'll have to kill you."

Paul shook his head and laughed at my explanation.

"Yanks," he said. "You guys sure know how to muck up a perfect language."

"How can it be so perfect if you call the game of soccer football?" I asked.

Clyde rose to his feet and stepped between us on his way to the barn.

"Nice work," Paul said as he gave Clyde a pat on the side.

"I guess Clyde's calling it a wrap," John said.

We retired to the house to take a look at the death scene. If they handed out Oscars to camels for perfect acting, Clyde would be on his way to Hollywood today.

There was one final scene to film to complete for the segment at Camelot, but it didn't involve camels. To tie in the saber tooth, they needed a large cat. Mountain lions are the apex predators in the West, but where could we find a mountain lion on such short notice?

"Tell you what," I said. "Let's feed the camels and head into town. If you buy me lunch, I'll introduce you to Kika."

"Who is Kika?" Paul asked.

"Kika is the most beautiful cougar you've ever seen," I said. "The best part is she lives in Moab."

"Any chance you've got a saber tooth in town too?" John said.

"It's not in your budget," I answered. "But I bet that Kika is."

An hour later, the three of us headed over the long, bumpy road to Moab in search of lions.

Kika

THE LAST DAY of filming camels at the lodge was a momentous occasion. All of the animals had performed beyond my wildest expectations. Clyde, of course, had proven himself to be an exceptional animal actor. There was much to celebrate. Bill, Moto, Cefa, Curly, Raji, and Gwennie were all given a special treat that morning. A giant fruit salad was served with all their favorites were included. Apples, bananas, watermelon, and cantaloupe as well as a fifty-pound bag of carrots – all compliments of BBC.

*   *   *

Tomorrow Kika would arrive, and I had no idea how she would react to her new setting at Camelot. Her story was a tragic tale of ignorance and greed. She and her two siblings were born wild.

The La Sal Mountains above Moab were home to a variety of wildlife. Deer, elk, black bears, and cougars all called this spectacular range their home. It was also a favorite recreation area for the locals. Several lakes in the La Sal Mountains offered trout fishing, and hunters from throughout the state flocked to the open meadows and forests to hunt mule deer and trophy elk.

In spite of their self-appointed title as nature lovers, some sportsmen considered competition from wild predators unacceptable. The laws protecting the lions, bears, and coyotes and other meat eaters were often flagrantly disregarded; and any varmints unlucky enough to be caught in the crosshairs were usually shot on sight.

It was early spring, and the mother mountain lion was crossing an open meadow dangerously close to a paved road. A man in the camouflage jacket spotted the cougar family from the front seat of his truck. He immediately pulled off onto the shoulder and grabbed the 30 Remington AR that was in its usual spot, hanging in the gun rack in the rear window. A box of one-hundred-and-eighty-grain shells was stashed in the glove box within easy reach. This was the moment he lived for: an easy kill from the front seat of his truck. What he didn't realize, however, was a family returning from a camping trip had also spotted the mountain lions and were parked along a dirt road, hoping to get a once-in-a-lifetime photograph of a family of wild cougars.

When the shot rang out, the mother lion dropped to the ground, writhing in pain. The poacher's aim was deadly and accurate. The two young cubs crouched behind their dying mother, uncertain of what had happened.

The woman in the RV was shocked and outraged by what she had just witnessed. She jumped from the truck screaming and began waving her arms in the air. A second shot rang out, and the male cub was killed instantly. It was at that moment the cowardly man realized his slaughter of the mother lion and her cub had been witnessed. One cub was still alive, but he dared not risk being caught. He would have liked to take his trophy home with him. The boys in Hanksville loved hearing about lions being killed. They figured the deer and elk belonged to them, so every time a cougar made a kill, there would be one less trophy deer head for their dens.

The 1987 Dodge pickup would be easy to identify. Looking through his binoculars, the man in the RV could easily read the license plate. As he jotted the tag number on a paper sack, he pulled out his cell phone and called for help. The signal was faint, but the 911 operator was able to decipher the frantic call and relayed the message to the local sheriff's department.

The infant cat cowered behind his now-dead mother. The dark red blood covered her tawny coat and soaked the grass beneath her body. Terrified, the lone survivor of the tragic massacre called out to her lifeless brother. His head had nearly been severed by the powerful weapon, and her pleading calls went unanswered.

The grief-stricken woman approached cautiously. She could hear her husband's warning to keep back.

"A wounded animal protecting her young could be doubly dangerous," he said. In her lifetime of raising horses and cattle, she knew the risks, but her motherly instinct to protect the cub overrode her fear. Sensing that the mother lion was dead, she sat quietly in the tall grass, whispering reassurances to the frightened kitten. Her husband approached his distraught wife quietly.

"Where are the kids?" she asked.

"There in the truck," he answered.

"Don't let them see this."

"Of course not," he said. "I got the asshole's license number."

A white truck was cruising slowly down the deserted road. The emblem on the door read Department of Fish and Wildlife. The man waved to the game warden and walked briskly toward the approaching vehicle. Rudy, the warden, exited the truck and walked in the direction of the sorrowful man in the meadow.

"Are you the one that called?" he asked.

"Yes," he replied. "Thank you for coming. He just started shooting. The mother and one cub are dead, but one baby is still alive. My wife is out there keeping an eye on it."

The ranger was all too familiar with crimes against wildlife. He was often required to testify in court against the perpetrators. Most were never apprehended, but those that were caught often went on to repeat their heinous acts.

"Did you see who did this?" Rudy asked.

"Yes, I got his license number and a description of the vehicle."

Before the helpful camper could finish his description of the old pickup, Rudy knew who the man was. That hunting guide had a long rap sheet on file for hunting violations such as poaching, hunting out of season, spotlighting animals at night, and even shooting animals in state and national parks.

"I know who he is," Rudy said. "Would you be willing to testify in court?"

Without a moment's hesitation, the man answered, "Absolutely, we both will."

"Maybe this time we can put him away," Rudy said.

When they got to the woman sitting in the grass, they could see she had been crying. Her eyes were red and moist, and streaks on her dusty cheeks revealed her deep sorrow for the senseless deaths.

"Why do people do this to animals?" she asked.

The man with the badge had no answers. Twenty-two years of witnessing the waste and destruction of wildlife was more than he could handle. He would retire in a year's time, but the nightmares would remain with him for the duration of his life.

"Not all hunters are like this," Rudy said. "Most are honest, responsible sportsman. A few are just bad apples."

He returned to his truck to retrieve a large plastic dog kennel and a pair of thick cowhide gloves. The surviving lion cub would be kept as evidence. But then the real dilemma would be locating someone willing and qualified to care for the little orphan cougar cub.

I received a call from Rudy on Sunday morning. The story was heartbreaking when he asked me if I knew of someone willing to foster the orphan. One name immediately came to mind. My friend Charlie Avery lived in Moab. He and I had talked about building a nature center, and there was no question in my mind Charlie and his wife, Becky, would gladly take in the cub. He had not worked with wild animals but had good instincts. Most of all, he had a heart of gold.

We drove to Salt Lake the next morning to fill out the forms required to become wildlife rehabilitation facility. A week later, the young cougar was placed in our care. With Becky's nurturing spirit and Charlie's natural ability to interact with animals, the young cougar began the long process of healing.

Within a matter of weeks, she was romping in her pen with her adopted family and joining Charlie and his border collie on long walks into the vast desert surrounding their home. The heroes responsible for saving the animal's life stopped by to visit the growing cub. They informed us the man responsible for shooting the mother cougar and her kitten was captured and jailed. He was currently awaiting trial. They were elated to see the orphan in such loving hands but were somewhat disappointed to learn she would never be released back into the wild. By the human imprint of her caregivers, Kika would lose her natural fear of humans and could potentially be killed if she encountered a group of campers or deer hunters. Kika would never live out her life in the mountains where she was born. Hopefully, she could grow up as an ambassador for her species. Future generations of humans could develop a greater appreciation for the wildlife of North America. That goal was already in progress.

In the end, countless schoolchildren in the Moab area would hear the story of the orphaned cougar cub and most would grow to love her. As for Kika, in spite of her tragic beginning, she was growing into a beautiful and trusting cat that thrived in her new life with the family who adored her.

Kika's Debut

KIKA ARRIVED BY boat. Sitting contentedly on Charlie's lap, she hung over the edge of the small skiff and batted at the waves churned up by the outboard. Pulling up to an exposed sandbar, Charlie set the anchor and walked up to the road leading to the house. So far, the trip was fairly uneventful. That changed when Kika caught sight of the camels grazing in the pasture. At first, she froze in place, wondering what terrible and frightening creatures these must be. The camels paid no attention to the frightened cougar and continued grazing on the few remaining tumbleweeds left in the open meadow.

Charlie knelt down next to the anxious cat and stroked her silky coat. But all the reassuring words Charlie could think of were not enough to convince Kika to budge. It donned on me that Kika's best friend in the world, next to Charlie, was his little border collie, Daisy Mae. Perhaps Jinda could redirect her attention and convince the half-grown lion not to worry about the camels. In order to do that, I would have to convince Jinda not to worry about the lion.

I should have known my little cattle dog trusted me. I would never knowingly put her life in danger, and without hesitation, Jinda followed me to the road where Charlie and Kika were waiting. The moment the nervous cub spotted Jinda, the camels were instantly forgotten. Kika's complete attention was focused on the dog.

"Hit the sack, Jinda," I said.

The command was to Jinda indicated a special treat was waiting for her in her bed. Spinning on a dime, she headed back toward the house at full speed to retrieve her reward, and hot on her heels was Kika with Charlie in tow. Once again, my wonderful dog had saved the day. Upon reaching the porch, Kika lost interest in the dog and instead curled up in the shade to survey her new surroundings. John

197

and Paul, the crew from BBC, were ecstatic to have a live mountain lion for their film. But now the true test came.

The filmmakers hiked to a secluded slot canyon adjacent to the property for the first shot with Kika. For the first time since her rescue, Kika would be running free. If her bond with Charlie was as strong as we hoped it was, everything would go smoothly. If not, there would be little hope of catching her.

I rigged up a lure of shredded cloth on the end of a fishing pole. By casting the bundle of rags and jerking it erratically along the ground, we might keep the cougar interested in chasing the toy, and we could pull this whole thing off. We were about to find out.

When we entered the coolness of the narrow canyon, Kika's excitement increased. The distinct tracks of bighorn sheep, mule deer, and rabbits littered the canyon floor. Mountain lions, like Kika, had hunted these secret arroyos for eons; and in spite of her gentle nature, Kika was still a wild animal. Her instinct told her that this was a place where she belonged.

Kiowa a smaller cousin to the Mountain Lion

Charlie offered her a chunk of fresh venison, and she gently took it from his fingers. When that was gone, Kika looked up, intently hoping for more. This would be to our advantage. If the lure failed, perhaps the raw meat would keep her nearby. The time had come to begin filming.

"Roll camera," John whispered.

With a nod to Charlie, I crossed my fingers as the chain around Kika's neck was removed. The young mountain lion glanced up at the steep canyon walls, uncertain as to what to do. I cast the rag lure in her direction and began jigging it along the canyon floor. Playfully, the tawny cat pounced toward its quarry, missing by inches. Running backward, I scurried past the camera crew, Kika close behind.

"Brilliant, absolutely brilliant," John said.

Kika had now performed her first role on film, and she had done so completely free. Charlie came over and offered the new film star another taste of meat, and she eagerly devoured the tidbit.

"Let's go," he said, trotting back up the canyon. Kika followed like a faithful dog. For the remainder of the day, she ran freely through the desert and canyons, never losing sight of her trusted friend. When the filming was completed that evening, Kika walked calmly back to the ranch. At the top of a sandy ridge, she gazed down on the small band of camels standing in their pens, nibbling on hay. This time, however, she exhibited no hesitation and walked confidently past the camels without so much as glancing in their direction. The world and its inhabitants were no longer a threat to Kika. In spite of her terrifying introduction to the human race, those who surrounded her now looked upon with the utmost love and admiration.

In all my years of working animals in movies and commercials, I had never experienced such grace and beauty as we did on that day. Kika would return to the quiet canyons around Camelot on many more occasions, but not to work. There were miles and miles of unexplored wilderness around the lodge. A perfect playground for Kika and Charlie and the freedom she would experience there would set her wild spirit free.

After airing on both BBC and Discovery Channel, *Wild New World* brought Camelot into the twenty-first century. Film crews became a regular fixture at the lodge. Animal Planet was producing a new show called *Get Out There*, which included a camel ride for a wonderful family from Chicago. Discovery Channel returned with *Man vs. Wild*. Although camels were not featured in the segment, the lodge and its beautiful backdrop were.

Next to follow were *Ms. Adventure* and a PBS special on the six best backcountry lodges in North America. I also received calls for, of all things, two adult films, but declined. Guests were arriving at Camelot almost daily for hikes in the backcountry riverboat excursions and, of course the crème dela crème, a world-class camel ride to the wind caves and beyond.

Going Solo

Solo the wandering dog

THERE WILL ALWAYS be ups and downs in any business venture. It's part of life. But when working with animals, the biggest downside is the sad reality we will probably outlive most of our beloved pets. Because camels have an average life span of about fifty years, there was a good chance I wouldn't have to suffer through another tragic loss with my four-legged animal friends. Though there was, of course, one exception: my wonderful friend Jinda.

She was beginning to show the signs of a dog beyond her prime. The obvious slight graying on her muzzle and her energy escaping a little sooner than usual on our long camel treks. Although she was no longer able to outrun the pesky ground squirrels when they raided the vegetable garden, she was still the light of my life. I refused to think about her passing on to the next life where she would, no doubt, bring a greater joy to the angels that sent her to me.

One day, one of my guests made a suggestion that getting another dog might be helpful in putting a little spring back in Jinda's step. At first, I rejected the idea; but after giving the dog/duo idea more thought, I realized the numerous benefits of getting a new younger companion for my best friend. A few days later after taking a young Ohio couple back to town after their two-day honeymoon at Camelot, I opted to take the paved potash road home. I kept my canoe stashed in the bushes on the opposite side of the river. That particular day, my back wasn't feeling up to the long bumpy road home, so the canoe was perfect for just an occasion.

As I neared the old campground, which had once been my temporary home when this whole escapade began, I saw something dart across the road ahead of me. At first, I thought it might have been a coyote. The size was about right, but the color was all wrong. I paused briefly to glance up the small canyon where the animal had disappeared but failed to immediately spot the elusive critter. Then I detected a slight movement a few hundred feet up the sandy wash. A small black-and-white border collie was lying in the shade of a large tamarisk tree. Visibly underweight and covered in mud, the dog had probably been dumped here for whatever reason.

I parked the truck in a small pullout alongside the road and walked back to get a closer look at the little orphan. If I was able to convince the dog to get in the truck, I could drive him back to town to the animal shelter where he could be looked after and put up for adoption. But the moment I rounded the corner, the little collie sprung to his feet and fled into the brush with his tail clamped firmly to his rump.

I returned to the area the following morning and once more spotted the lost animal sniffing around an old fire pit. This time, I brought something to entice the wary dog. I shook the bag of dog food out of the open truck window. Instead of fleeing, the frightened little dog took a few tentative steps in my direction. Placing a small plastic bowl on the ground outside the truck door, I drove a short distance down the road to see if the dog would eat the food. Solo (I dubbed him) was timid, but he was also starving. The few tidbits in the bowl were quickly wolfed down, and the still-hungry animal stood over the empty bowl, staring in my direction. All further attempts to lure the hungry dog closer were unsuccessful. At least, he wasn't running away.

After three long days of bringing food across the river to the frightened dog, I was still no closer to getting him anywhere near the truck. Something horrible had happened to this untrusting little dog, and a human was probably the cause. If there was any hope of capturing Solo, I would have to find another way, or eventually, he would be hit by a car or killed by coyotes. It was getting late and time to return home. I looked across the river toward the lodge and could see Jinda standing on a small sandbar on the opposite side, waiting for me.

Why hadn't I thought of this sooner? If anyone was capable of saving Solo, it would have to be his own kind. Humans had already proven themselves to be untrustworthy, but perhaps another dog could convince her to come home. At least, he would be safe and fed well. It was certainly worth a try. By the time I paddled the beat-up canoe back across the shallow river, Jinda anxiously greeted my arrival.

"Let's go save a dog," I said. Jinda jumped into the front seat, and I paddled the boat back to where I had just come. Solo was standing on a small knoll, watching us approach; and for the first time since I encountered this little dog, he was furiously wagging his tail.

"Go say hi," I said. Jinda trotted up the small hill, and the two animals greeted each other by sniffing and licking each other's face. The small handful of treats I stashed in my pockets was divided equally between the two animals. For the first time ever, I was able to gently stroke the lost dog's mangy fur. There was probably little hope of convincing Solo into the boat, but because the river was so low, he might try swimming across the river if Jinda would lead the way. I paddled out into the slow current and called to Jinda. A good swimmer since birth, she jumped into the shallow river and began working her way toward the opposite shore. Solo hesitated briefly but joined her newfound friend in what would hopefully be a new and more enriching life.

Solo settled in like he always belonged at Camelot. Within a few days, the gaunt little border collie began putting on weight, and a deep rich shine returned to the once-dull, lifeless coat. Two very unpleasant tasks were still at hand. One was giving Solo a good bath to rid the now-healthy dog of his foul smell. The second was a trip to the vet for vaccinations and neutering. I wasn't certain how easy it would be to get Solo into the truck, but once Jinda jumped into the backseat, Solo followed.

Everything about the little dog Solo was wonderful except for one very bad behavior. Solo liked to wander. This bad habit would need to change if he was to remain at the lodge. At first, Jinda remained on the property; but little by little, she also began to disappear for hours at a time. The dogs would always return home. But their long jaunts into the desert could, someday, have tragic consequences. Jinda was people friendly and could easily be lured into a stranger's car, never to be returned. There was also the possibility the dogs could be shot by a cattle rancher, bit by a snake, or injured in a fall. The next morning, I decided to take the appropriate steps to ensure the dogs' safety even if it required they both be tied up until the wandering faze ceased.

As it turned out, I would be one day too late in my plans, and Jinda would be nearly lost forever. It was late in the day with no sign of the two wandering dogs since early morning. I decided to take a drive toward Hurrah Pass to see if I could locate them before dark. As I rounded the first bend, I spotted Solo trotting down the road toward home. Jinda, however, was nowhere to be found. Solo continued looking back in the direction he had come and whined anxiously. The little dog was trying to tell me what had gone wrong that morning, but for the life of me, I couldn't understand his message.

I immediately returned home and began calling everyone who may be able to help me locate my lost dog. With the sun beginning to set, it would be futile to begin looking now and have to wait until morning. It would be a long, sleepless night; but at first light, I would scour the desert, looking for a dog that I loved dearly. Jinda meant more to me than most people I knew. She was far more than just a pet – she was family.

Some time after four in the morning, I dozed off. In my restless sleep, I could hear the mournful howl of my lost pet. The dream was so realistic that right before the sun rose over the anticline, I opened my eyes, listening intently. There it was. The distant but unmistakable cry only Jinda made. I knew it well because on the few occasions she had to be left at the vet's office or tied to the porch, she would raise her muzzle toward the heavens and let out the most pitiful moaning howl. This was a great relief. I knew that I could simply follow her cry and quickly locate my lost dog, but when I stepped onto the porch to get a bearing, the sound abruptly stopped.

Could I have just imagined her calls?

I went back inside to fill a water bottle, and within a few moments, the wailing began again. Back out on the porch, silence once more enveloped me. Wherever Jinda was, she could see me. I trained Jinda at an early age to quit barking when I was in sight. That training could now make finding her difficult, if not impossible. I quickly fed Solo and the camels and began my search toward the cliffs to the east. Somewhere out there was my lost dog, and I wouldn't rest until she was safely home.

For five long days, I searched in vain. I looked everywhere a lost dog could become stranded. On day 4, a group of eighteen volunteers arrived. These kindhearted individuals all assembled to help locate and hopefully bring Jinda safely home. I went so far as to hire a local helicopter to fly along the valley floor to assist in the search; but that evening, the haunting cries ceased, and I feared the worst. Friends and fellow searchers brought food and water out to me in the desert as I vowed not to return home without my dog. Right before the sun set over the western horizon on the fourth night, I detected one final mournful cry directly above me in the steep cliffs high above the valley floor.

I staggered home that night, too tired to continue. The following morning, I assembled the crew of rescuers, most of whom had come to the conclusion in spite of our efforts, Jinda would not be coming home. When we got to the base of the steep cliffs, I listened for any sounds of life. A single small stone tumbled down the cliff face. I desperately scrambled on all fours higher and higher up through the crumbling sandstone slope. Eventually, I could go no higher; and I collapsed on a small ledge, exhausted and brokenhearted. Jinda, I was certain, had died somewhere lost and alone; and it was all my fault. Suddenly, another rock tumbled from somewhere above me. Gazing up a hundred feet higher than any land mammal could climb, a small furry head peered over the cliff face.

"She's alive!" I yelled to the group huddled together below me.

"You stay there," someone shouted.

It was Larry Fisher. Larry was a good friend from Moab. He and his wife, Candy, were both avid climbers and loved dogs. They especially loved Jinda.

"We're going back to the road to see if we can find out how she got up there. Terry, you stay put and make sure she doesn't go anywhere. Don't worry we are going to get her down," they promised.

Almost a half mile toward Hurrah Pass, a faint but distinct bighorn sheep trail wound its way up through the boulders and fallen rock. From my vantage point, I watched Larry and Candy scramble higher and higher until they disappeared from view. They reappeared a short time later, walking along a narrow ledge at the base of the steep cliff face. By this time, it was obvious the two climbers were several hundred feet higher than my precarious perch and heading straight in the direction of my poor, stranded dog. Jinda began to whine, and tears began flowing from my eyes. When the heroic couple looked down at me from the narrow trail, no more than ten feet above Jinda's ledge, I knew the terrible ordeal was over. Larry carefully lowered his wife down to the exhausted dog. Candy took out a water bottle. Jinda lapped up the entire contents in a short amount of time. Next, Larry lowered a rope, and Candy fastened it around Jinda's shoulders. Working together, they pulled Jinda back up the trail, and the trio began retracing their steps back in the direction of home.

I don't really remember how I managed to scramble back down the road. Weeks later, I tried to get back to take a picture of Jinda's location, but I was unable to climb back to the spot where I first found her. It was suggested that Solo and Jinda had followed a band of wild bighorn sheep up the cliffs and Jinda either fell or was butted off the trail onto the small ledge where she would have died were it not for the heroic efforts of eighteen wonderful heroes. Thankfully, those individuals risked life and limb to help locate and rescue a very special little dog.

Although dehydrated and famished, Jinda couldn't resist the temptation to chase a squirrel down the hill the next morning right before jumping into my arms for the bumpy ride home. A big dinner and a firm but halfhearted scolding was a sufficient remedy to prevent this from happening again. Sadly, however, Solo would have to go.

One of the people aiding in the search was a young lady by the name of Rhonda. It seems she had been looking for a dog to adopt and had taken a particular liking to Solo. She had a big backyard – perfect for a pooch with wanderlust. Her yard was fully fenced, and since Solo seemed particularly smitten with Rhonda as well, the two departed Camelot hand in paw as happy as two peas in a pod.

I will forever be grateful to the small group of people, many of whom I had never met. My special thanks to Larry and Candy for bringing my dog home safely.

They will forever be my most treasured friends and two very special heroes I shall never forget.

Jinda learned her lesson. Thankfully, she never wandered off the ranch alone again but continued to lead the daily camel treks. Solo's new home was the perfect setting for the little border collie. Since Rhonda led an active lifestyle, Solo accompanied her almost everywhere she traveled and never again felt the need to wander.

* * *

Two more years passed without incident. A large growth on Jinda's side appeared almost overnight, and the decline in appetite and inability to move about the house without discomfort forewarned me in spite of all my hopes and prayers. Jinda was rapidly nearing the end of her life. I got three medical opinions, but each was the same. The tumor was inoperable, and the best I could hope for was a month's time.

One fateful morning, my special friend Jinda was no longer able to walk around the house. Holding her head in my lap, I drove into town where she was quietly laid to rest. There was a small outcropping above the lodge overlooking the Colorado River. It was her favorite place to lounge in the morning sun. From this vantage point, she could watch over the comings and goings of the ranch. I dug the grave. I placed her now-lifeless body on her favorite soft bed and sobbed uncontrollably. Stones were placed in a mound to mark the site and prevent predators from digging up the grave. I erected a small cross to serve as a headstone.

For the next few weeks, I would wander far into the surrounding desert. Every canyon, every sand dune, and every fleeing ground squirrel would remind me of the incredible joy this wonderful dog brought into my life. These memories, however, could not help mend my broken heart. I still had three of my favorite camels:, Clyde, Bill, and my youngest, Gwennie. But even these cherished friends could not rekindle my will to carry on. Camelot was no longer the place of my dreams, and I needed time to heal. A place somewhere far from the painful memories that now surrounded me.

In two short weeks, though, three amazing things would happen that would change my life entirely. The first was a young couple who called to arrange a camel ride. Sam Savoy and his wife, Erin, had been looking to start a small camel-trekking business in the Denver area. They were hoping to test-ride my camels but also hoped they could buy them. After several days of visiting with the couple, I came to realize their hearts were in the right place and agreed to visit their small farm in the Rifle area. The first thing became perfectly clear when I stepped into their modest home. These were animal people. The cats and dogs were more than just pets. They were part of their family. Even the horses they boarded for income were treated with love and kindness. At the end of my brief visit, I decided to make the Savoys an offer that would help them pursue their dreams and free me up to travel to some of the remote destinations I had always dreamed of.

"How would you like to adopt the camels for a short time?" I suggested. "See if owning camels is really what you're looking for."

I need some time away, and in a few months, we can sit down and figure out where to go from there. The wannabe cameleers were ecstatic and immediately agreed to the arrangement. They would be required to provide a good home for the trio, and I would spend the necessary amount of time training them in the art of camel wrangling. Gwennie, Bill, and Clyde would be visiting Colorado until I could make the necessary plans for our future.

Camelot would sadly be put up for sale. I was ready to seek out the next great adventure. It was selfish, but ultimately lifesaving. Winter was coming, and spending so much time alone surrounded by the memories of so much loss was more than I could bear. The following week, Sam loaded all that was dear to me into the long stock trailer, and we headed east to Colorado.

A friend from Moab would keep an eye on things at the ranch while I joined Sam and Erin in Rifle to get the animals adjusted to their new temporary home. No sooner had the truck and trailer departed for Colorado when a phone call came in from my old friend and realtor Randy Day. After a few moments of small talk, Randy got down to the reason for calling.

"Terry," he said, "I have a gentleman arriving in town tomorrow from San Diego. He's looking for a remote parcel of land to purchase to build a little guest lodge for him and his business partners. The first thing I thought of was Camelot. Are you planning on spending the rest of your life stuck out there in the boonies? Or would you consider meeting with this guy to see if it's something worth looking into?"

My reply would either be the answer to my prayers or the worst decision I had ever made.

"I'll have to sleep on it, Randy," I said though sleep would be a long time coming that night. I knew the time had come to set out on a new adventure, but everything around me begged me to stay. Camelot had been my home for ten years. That was longer than I had ever remained in the same place in my entire life.

"God," I said, "if you can hear my prayers, lead me in the right direction one last time." The decision I made that night would indeed send me down a path that would forever change my life, and it would be a decision I would never regret.

The Land of Legends

An amazing sunset over the Amazon Rainforest

T HE SMALL CREEK that branched off the Tyayo River was one of many tributaries winding their way down to eventually feed into the mighty Amazon River.

On this sultry July morning, a mist still hung in the air. The pouring rain had ceased its deluge. As we bailed the water from the bottom of the canoe, we peered through the dense foliage. We listened intently for some sound or signal to tell us we were at last on the right track. The prize we sought was an apex predator in this region. Adult anacondas were both feared and respected by every creature that lived here.

Even the jaguar, largest of all the jungle cats, thought twice about entering these murky waters. Any lingering scent in the air to indicate an anaconda had passed this way always caused concern. The large black caiman was far less wary and had recently fallen victim to its reptilian cousin. Local villagers warned the children who fished in the hand-hewn dugout canoes to always look carefully before entering the water.

"A snake may be lurking there," they'd say. "If she finds you, she may devour you!"

The barking cry of a giant river otter was heard far upstream, but reason for the alarm was uncertain. All the conditions were right that morning. Towing the small two-man craft behind us, we began our voyage. As the equatorial sun filtered through the trees, a great sense of adventure overwhelmed me.

"At last," I said aloud, "the home of the mighty anaconda."

Even before reaching puberty, I had dreamed of traveling to the Amazon basin. The abundance of life here was overwhelming. Countless documentaries filmed in this vast region gave viewers a brief glimpse into the numerous newly discovered bird, insect, and mammal species that existed here. But my dream focused not on the colorful birds or fishes, but the amazing reptiles. One in particular held my fascination – the green anaconda.

Legendary but undocumented reports told of snakes attaining lengths sixty feet and a thousand pounds had circulated throughout the Amazon for decades. Skins measuring more than forty feet occasionally surfaced. These were usually sold and sometimes displayed in the city shops surrounding the jungle. But the remarkable elasticity of a snake skin is the probable cause for the giant skins.

Captive snakes, however, can grow to lengths of thirty-three feet; and wild serpents weighing several hundred pounds have been captured. Even larger anacondas that have come close to or have exceeded the impressive records do possibly exist somewhere deep in the jungles of South America. The giants of all giants live safely far from the cities and remote villages. The only predator capable of destroying this remarkable creature is mankind. He is one of the few creatures on earth who destroys another species without logic, rhyme, or reason.

The small tributary was already showing great promise. The dusky red palm snakes and Amazon tree boas had already made their presence known. My guide and good friend Orlando had grown up in this region and was an expert jungle-trained naturalist. He could identify almost any mammal, bird, or insect just by listening to the faintest of sounds or observing a track along a muddy bank. We met a few months earlier when I briefly visited the Amazon. I had hopes of finding a suitable location and an experienced guide for my admittedly harebrained scheme of capturing a green anaconda.

Who knows what makes us take the sometimes-unexplainable journeys we embark on. For me, capturing a giant snake made perfect sense. Of the previous excursions I had into Central America, I found Indonesia and India always had the same theme – snakes. But this was not just any snake, this serpent was legendary. When I discussed my goals with Orlando, he too shared in the excitement. His expertise would not only increase our chances of locating a snake, but there could be no better companion to ensure we would both make it out of here alive.

A trio of Jaguar Cubs

Two baby black caimen rescued from fish net

There were plenty of fish swimming in the deep pools. The predatory peacock bass, arawanas, and oscars could be seen lying in wait for smaller prey species. With a little luck, an anaconda might be discovered lying in wait for them. Although fish was the primary diet of small anacondas, the adults were accomplished ambush predators. The largest of specimens were capable of subduing and swallowing most of the birds and mammals that became careless enough to stumble into their lair. Once the great coils of these massive snakes enveloped their intended prey, there would be no tomorrow.

"What makes you think there might be a snake in this creek?" I asked Orlando.

We had toiled up this log-strewn creek for more than an hour. Being accustomed to the equatorial sun, I was almost suffocated by the stifling heat. I was already dreading the equally daunting task of the return trip. A fisherman we briefly visited with on the Tyayo River had apparently informed Orlando that two days previously, he had seen the tracks of a large snake at the entrance to the stream. Another villager he had spoken to had actually seen the snake. That man advised us to avoid the area recently because of it.

It appeared that everyone in the entire region was already aware of the fact a very large snake was living somewhere up this creek. That is everyone but me!

Amazon

Deep in the heart of the camp wide rainforest

A NACONDAS, LIKE GIANT snakes everywhere, are often enveloped in a shroud of myth and legend. Ancient stories depict these serpents as almost godlike. But there are many gods. Good gods as well as evil ones. The snake can be either. Medical symbols reveal the snake as a healer whereas the Bible aligns the snake with Satan. It is neither the snakes' good or evil symbolism that threatens the survival of the giant anaconda.

Snake skins, especially those of this proportion, are sought out for mere trophies. Sadly, local villagers encountering these regal serpents knew the skins could fetch a month's wages. In the bustling city of Iquitos, located in the heart of the jungle, local business owners adorned their shop walls with anaconda hides. These massive snakes were rapidly disappearing. The good news was eco-friendly tourists can and do make a difference. By letting business owners know you will no longer support those who displayed live animals or their skins as wall ornaments, the demand for these snakes diminished. Even the roadside shows that illegally collected wildlife to hustle tourist dollars had to seek employment elsewhere when visitors set the example by walking away.

*   *   *

As we rested briefly on a sandbar, Orlando shared a little of his family history. He grew up in the Amazon rainforest. He had, in fact, never left his jungle home. Orlando was my guide. He knew this region intimately, but the remainder of the world was a mystery. I wondered to myself if he ever dreamed of traveling to other lands as I did. Would a trip, say to Disneyland, forever extinguish his gentle and unhurried spirit? Ignorance is bliss, or so it's been said. I've met few people in my life who seem less ignorant, but so filled with bliss as Orlando. He hunted these waterways with his father for bush meat. As a young boy, it was his staple diet. Meals in the Amazon come from one of two sources: what you hunt or what you grow. The thin topsoil makes farming tedious and produces little. But life abounds.

"What would you hunt?" I inquired.

"Many things," he answered. "The agouti is my favorite."

Agoutis are jackrabbit-sized rodents. Mainly nocturnal, they are usually caught in wire snares.

"White-lipped peccaries are a delicacy here," he added.

Peccaries are small piglike mammals, which are South American cousins to the Arizonan javelina. Traveling in bands of thirty or more, their sharp tusks and poor eyesight make them a formidable adversary. They dine on fallen fruit, nuts, and insects but will also prey on small mammals and reptiles. The long, pronounced scars on Orlando's calf were subtle reminders of one such encounter with a peccary and a painful lesson. When you enter these forests, you're never alone.

*   *   *

The midmorning heat had intensified. We lounged in a deep pool beneath a massive mahogany. Demand for this valuable lumber has reduced most of these trees, and the machete notch in this one indicated it too would be harvested by summer's end. Small fish darted from their shelter under the tree's roots to nibble on my leg hairs as Orlando recalled stories from the past. Another irreplaceable giant species was losing its struggle to survive.

"There were black caiman in this lake when I was very small," he said. "Some were more than two meters long. We shot a tapir in that clearing many years ago."

As he explained, he pointed to a small opening in the forest across the shallow lake.

"It was the last one living in this region. The Baird's tapir is a distant relative of elephants. They were once common here, and an adult tapir could feed an entire village. But there are many more villages now, and the tapirs are gone."

*   *   *

"When I was around seven years old," he said, "I remember seeing an anaconda not far from here. It was as long as the boat ramp at the lodge."

I recalled passing a long wooden boat dock earlier in the day, which jutted far out into the river. I calculated the ramp to be at least fifty feet long. Surely, no anaconda ever attained such a massive length, but the memories he shared with me were special. I felt honored he would share these treasured memories with me.

It was an anaconda we were looking for. The purpose for this hopeful journey was to capture one of these great serpents and hold its writhing coils in my hands before releasing it unharmed. It was an adventure I dreamed of since childhood. Perhaps today, that dream would at last come true.

We began toiling upstream. As we dragged the cumbersome canoe up the small waterway, I wondered if we would indeed find the giant snake we were seeking. Although this was the ideal habitat for snakes, it was, in no way, the ideal habitat for us. Fish, a primary food source for anacondas, were plentiful here. Orlando pointed out the small tracks of the agouti rats and other small mammals on the muddy banks. Any snake that lived long enough to grow to a fifteen-foot specimen we hoped to find would be wary. By slipping silently beneath the muddy water, she could glide effortlessly between the tangle of roots and vines, avoiding our detection. It would be my good luck and Orlando's great skill if we were to be granted an audience with this legendary serpent.

"*Por que* [Why] are we looking only for snakes?" Orlando asked me.

"Not just snakes, Orlando, anacondas," I replied.

"Most tourists come here to see birds or monkeys," he said. "We usually avoid the snakes."

"If you were a tourist," I asked him, "what would you want to see?"

"Snakes," he replied.

"Good, Orlando, then let's keep looking."

"Alto! I mean stop," he corrected, forgetting for a moment my Spanish was very limited. A large coil appeared on the surface directly ahead of us. My heart was racing, and adrenaline surged through my veins. In my excitement, I lunged forward. The moment had come at last, I thought. Before it slipped beneath the murky water, I saw the color of the snake, but it was not what I was expecting. But what else would come close to having such large coils? Grabbing my arm, Orlando motioned me back into my seat.

"Did you see the size of that snake?" I asked him, barely able to contain my excitement.

"No," he chuckled. "But did you see the size of those electric eels?"

They rose again to the surface now barely ten feet away. Their writhing bodies intertwined in what – I can only assume – was some sort of mating ritual. Still laughing, Orlando reminded me in a Spanish word I knew well.

"No *tacto*. [Do not touch.] And no *beso*. [Don't kiss.]" he added.

Electric eels could pack a whooping fifty thousand volts of electricity, so I thought about two things: What would the combined one hundred thousand volts of electricity do to me if I had been foolish enough to grab them, and would the voltage kill me outright or just curl my hair? Second thought was more of a curiosity. How in the hell do these things breed?

Slapping the water with our paddles, the eels ceased their courtship and slithered by us back in the direction we had just come.

"I hope we see them on the way home," Orlando joked. He looked at me to see my reaction.

"Doesn't matter to me," I shot back. "I'll be in the canoe. Remember, you're the guide. By the way, Orlando, are you a religious man?" I said sternly.

Some of the color had faded from his face. "I am today," he replied.

Around the next bend in the stream, a lake suddenly appeared. My disappointment could not have been more apparent.

"If there was an anaconda in this lake, we won't ever find her," I announced in dismay.

"Maybe, we can find her in the shallows," he said.

"What shallows?" I asked. The lake appeared to be deep and dark along its entire perimeter.

"Other side," he said, pointing to the distant shoreline.

"And how do we get there?" I whined. My adrenaline from the eel sighting was fading fast, and the sun was now directly overhead. There would be no mahogany trees to block the intense heat and glaring rays.

"Same way we got here." Orlando smiled and splashed water in my direction.

"Let's take a break," I suggested. Grabbing a paddle, we headed for a nearby tributary that was entering the lake from the east.

"Feel like swimming with the eels?" Orlando asked. The color had returned to his face.

"I'll be right behind you, pard," I answered. "It's an adventure, right?"

Tall grass lined the bank in the shallow inlet as I stepped confidently from the tipsy canoe. The water was crystal clear here.

"Shh!"

I looked up at my trusty guide. He was pointing at the bank. Thinking this to be a prank, I looked back at Orlando.

"Anaconda," he said. The look on his face told me at once this was no prank. Barely visible in the thick grass, the snake was perhaps eight feet long and lying partially submerged.

"Probably, a male," I surmised. The tail was longer than a female's anaconda would be, and the head was narrower. The iridescent green scales shone in the sunlight, and the excitement returned. An anaconda at last. I moved slowly, approaching the snake from the rear. The rapidly flicking tongue left little doubt the snake was unaware of our presence. Surprisingly, it made an attempt to escape. Hoping the capture would not traumatize the snake, I gently slid my hands beneath his body. There was no reaction.

Great, this is going to be easy, I thought.

As I lifted the snake slowly from the lake, its head turned to face me, and I felt its body stiffen. The flicking tongue now moved toward my hand. The strike was so sudden. I had no time to respond. The hundred or so needle-sharp teeth clamped down on my hand, and his coils began to tighten around my arm.

Don't panic, I told myself. This was not the first time a large constrictor had drawn blood from my hand. Orlando leapt from the boat with a machete in hand.

"No!" I shouted.

Orlando stopped in his tracks. I remained motionless, and the snake began to release its grip on my bleeding hand. The snake refocused on a new target. The second strike missed my face by inches, but before I could drop the agitated serpent back in the lake, he latched firmly on my soggy trousers.

"Get the camera," I shouted to my bewildered companion, "before he finds something else to chew on!"

There was no longer any flesh in the angry snake's mouth, just fabric; but apparently, he still wasn't letting go. I was certain the snake would soon inflict another painful bite, so I did the only logical thing I could think of. I removed my pants. So as Orlando clicked away with the camera, I dropped the entire package of snake and britches back into the water. I remained quietly on the bank half-naked, but thoroughly elated. Eventually, the snake released its prize and glided away into deeper water. Once the snake detached itself from my apparel, it disappeared beneath the surface of the lake and would never reappear. The dream was every bit as grand as I had imagined, and I was elated at having seen and momentarily captured my first wild, beautiful South American anaconda.

To my relief, the large female anaconda we sought from the beginning was never located. Eight feet of feisty snake was all the adventure I could handle that day. The small circular tear in my cotton britches served as a reminder to follow the advice of herpetologist worldwide: mess with anacondas and you are going to get bit. Next time, I will keep my hands to myself and use my zoom lens.

Only three people have or will ever see the pictures Orlando took of our great adventure: me, my guide and great friend Orlando, and the totally confused stranger who developed the film.

God's Greatest Gift

HUMANS ARE A gregarious species. We live our lives for the most part surrounded by our own kind. I, on the other hand, sought comfort and solace from other species even as a child. It is true I was never a recluse locked away in a wilderness cabin avoiding the human race, but there has been what might be considered an invisible wall built around me. Its construction began at an early age and was anchored firmly in place throughout much of my lifetime. I was largely unaware of its presence until little by little, brick by brick the wall began to crumble.

The sometimes-harsh and cruel world that builds such walls can, it turns out, be painlessly unraveled by the most gentle and loving hands.

The Value of Life

THE FINAL CHAPTER in our own lives will be the completion of our own circle. So my thoughts here are intended more as a self-examination than a message to others. Any wisdom that I may have acquired along my journey will reflect on the footprints that I leave behind.

So if, as spiritual leaders suggest, my redemption can only be attained through atonement, then I too must mend my own circle by following the examples of the teachers who brought me here. I will begin now.

It is both a blessing and a curse to be given such an important task of being stewards of the earth – responsible for all life that exists upon it.

So I would conclude my circle is not truly mine alone but intricately linked to all others. My mere presence here does not validate my right to exist as a single link but is, in fact, part of a chain contained within the circle as a whole. My everyday actions or reactions can affect or even eliminate a host of other creatures.

So how then do I atone?

Would the creator of all life thank me in the end for correcting his or her mistakes? Or is it, as I suspect, nature without the interference of humankind that is truly flawless?

A great teacher in my own life learned a valuable lesson from listening to the heart of his student. As a young boy, I watched in horror as my uncle Joe committed an unforgivable crime. A great man, by all accounts, shot a coyote, which was harmlessly crossing an open field. In the late afternoon, the hay behind the small farmhouse in the red-rock country of Price, Utah, was cut and drying in rows.

A coyote was searching for field mice and voles to feed her growing pups. The very man who proclaimed his daily allegiance to a god that, by his own testimony, created all living things destroyed a miracle of life in less time than it would take to locate the chapter and verse in the Holy Bible he carried by his side.

Did not those same biblical passages forbid it?

"Will God thank you for correcting his mistakes?" I asked him.

"God doesn't make mistakes," he replied.

He hadn't really taken the time to ponder the question that I had asked him. But perhaps during his nightly prayers, he had. By morning, the rifle was no longer above the kitchen doorway where it was kept. Had my uncle given deeper thought to his response?

"God doesn't make mistakes."

Later that summer, his true wisdom shone through when he explained to me his own childhood teachers in error taught him. The difference between man and beast is that animals exist without conscience.

"I would now beg to differ," he continued. "It appears that only mankind destroys life for his own convenience."

On that special day, my great uncle Joe became not only my teacher but my hero.

CPSIA information can be obtained at www.ICGtesting.com
Printed in the USA
BVOW080528311012

304220BV00001B/3/P